D0530429

Caribbean
Cuisine

By
Dr. Betty "K"

**Exotic Island Flavours
Simple, Easy-to-Prepare Recipes**

Front Cover:
Crab Backs, page 16
Planter's Punch, page 25

Caribbean Cuisine
by
Dr. Betty K

Second Printing — June 1991

Canadian Cataloguing in Publication Data

K., Betty, —
Caribbean cuisine

ISBN: 0-919845-77-0

1. Cookery, Caribbean.   I. Title.
TX 716.A1K2   1990   641.59729   C90-097017-0

Glass plates created by glass artist Kelly Brown
Fragile Art Works, Vancouver, B.C.

Photography by:
Patricia Holdsworth
Patricia Holdsworth Photography
Regina, Saskatchewan

Designed, Printed and Produced in Canada by:
Centax Books, a Division of M•C•Graphics Inc.
Publishing Director, Photo Designer and Food Stylist: Margo Embury
1048 Fleury Street, Regina, Saskatchewan, Canada   S4N 4W8
(306) 359-3737   Fax (306) 525-3955

Table of Contents

Introduction

Years of entertaining relatives and friends, in many parts of the world, have inspired me to write this book on Caribbean Cuisine.

I was born in Georgetown, Guyana, a former British Colony located on the northern coast of South America. I pursued undergraduate studies at McGill University, Montreal, then went on to study Medicine at the Royal College of Surgeons in Dublin, Ireland. I have lived and practiced in Ireland, England, Trinidad, Guyana and Canada. I lived in Toronto for 7 years, then in the Province of Saskatchewan for 12 years, where I started this book.

During my years as a student and a physician I have travelled many times to the Caribbean and have collected recipes from the islands I visited. Some of my Guyanese recipes were given to me by my mother, who helped me to expand my culinary skills. Indeed, we in the Caribbean are very proud of our cuisine and we take great delight in preparing and presenting our meals.

The recipes in this book retain the exotic flavours of the islands and take you on an international tour of many cultures. These recipes are adapted to my busy lifestyle.

Most of the ingredients are available at large North American supermarkets, and others are available at Oriental and West Indian grocery stores. I hope that you enjoy this taste of the Caribbean and take pleasure in sharing it with family and friends.

Bits and Pieces of the Caribbean

The Caribbean islands are sometimes referred to as the West Indies. Among these islands Columbus called the Indies there is a natural charm, the pace is slow and the mood is relaxed. In this book, we have concentrated on the cuisine of some of the English-speaking islands and Guyana, where the Caribbean Sea borders the East coast of Central America along the north coast of South America to Venezuela.

Throughout the Caribbean area, the temperature ranges between 70-85°F and with the Trade Winds blowing the inhabitants find it a tranquil and charming place to live.

Early Caribbean settlers were the Arawaks and Caribs who came from the American mainland and are now commonly called Amerindians. After Columbus opened up the Caribbean to Europe, people were needed to work in farming and in gold and silver exploration. In the 17th century when sugar production began, the labour force was provided by slaves from West Africa. After Britian made it illegal to trade in slaves, Indians and Chinese were persuaded to travel to the Caribbean as indentured workers. People came from afar and brought with them their traditional recipes and methods of cooking. They substituted available local ingredients in the preparation of their food.

Like the people and culture, Caribbean food is a mixture of characteristic flavours. This book captures the essence of Caribbean cooking secrets that were formerly passed down from generation to generation. The inevitable intermingling of the various cultures is also an important factor in the resulting cosmopolitan array of cuisines. The myriad local herbs and spices enliven every meal and, like the people and culture, produce a wonderful mixture of flavours. This marriage of flavours and cooking techniques from different parts of the world have been captured in the simple step-by-step recipes selected for Caribbean Cuisine.

by
Cecil Singh

Acknowledgement

I would like to thank my relatives and friends who have given me help and encouragement with this book.

My thanks to my mother, Mrs. R. Kissoon, who contributed recipes and helped me with the weights and measurements of ingredients in some of the recipes. Thanks to my children, David and Nadia for printing some of my recipes. Thanks to my sister-in-law, Vivian Singh, for her contributions and suggestions.

I would like to thank my friend, Patricia Fungon who contributed my Chinese recipes. My special thanks to my typists, my friend, Lil Lawford of Saskatoon, my daughter, Nadia Singh, and last but not least my friend, Sandra Moore, who completed my manuscript. My thanks to my friend, Audrey Sullivan, who introduced me to Centax Books and Margo Embury.

I would like to thank my husband, Cecil, for Bits and Pieces of the Caribbean, his encouragement and making this publication possible.

Map of the Caribbean

Appetizers, Condiments & Beverages

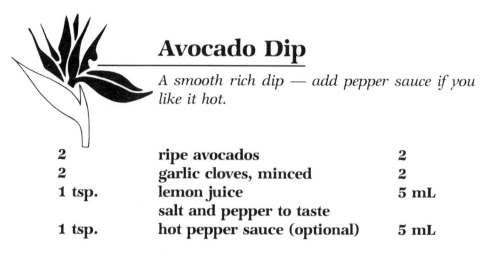

Avocado Dip

A smooth rich dip — add pepper sauce if you like it hot.

2	**ripe avocados**	2
2	**garlic cloves, minced**	2
1 tsp.	**lemon juice**	5 mL
	salt and pepper to taste	
1 tsp.	**hot pepper sauce (optional)**	5 mL

1. Peel avocados. Mash with a fork.
2. Stir in minced garlic, lemon juice, salt and pepper.
3. Add hot pepper sauce to taste and mix well.
4. Chill before serving. Serve with fresh vegetables, crackers or corn chips.

Yields 1 cup (250 mL)

Note: *The avocados should be firm but not hard.*

Variation: *Finely chopped ripe tomato adds colour and flavour.*

Pink Dip For Prawns

An attractive and piquant appetizer.

1 cup	**mayonnaise**	250 mL
2 tbsp.	**ketchup**	30 mL
1	**onion, grated**	1
1 tsp.	**vinegar**	5 mL
	salt and pepper to taste	
1	**minced garlic clove**	1
1 tsp.	**prepared mustard**	5 mL
1 tsp.	**hot pepper sauce (optional)**	5 mL

1. Combine all ingredients and blend well.
2. Chill before serving with cooked prawns.

Yields 1½ cups (375 mL)

Eggplant Chokha (Purée)

Guyana

Also known as aubergine, boulanger or melon-gene in some islands.

1	eggplant	1
1	garlic clove	1
1	small onion, chopped	1
	salt and pepper to taste	
1 tsp.	hot pepper sauce	5 mL
2 tsp.	cooking oil	10 mL

1. Make a slit about 1" (2.5 cm) long on each side of the eggplant.
2. Halve garlic clove and place 1 half in each slit.
3. Grill eggplant or barbecue until skin is tender and pulp is soft, about 20-30 minutes.
4. Remove from heat and peel skin from eggplant. Crush eggplant pulp and garlic. Add onion, salt, pepper and pepper sauce.
5. Heat the oil and pour over eggplant mixture; stir well. Serve warm or cold, with pita pockets for dipping into purée.

Yields 1 cup (250 mL).

The word "Guyana" means "land of the waters". It is the only English-speaking country in South America with a population of six races.

Egg Salad

The addition of dry mustard and pepper sauce enhances this perennial favourite.

6	hard-boiled eggs	6
1/2 cup	mayonnaise	125 mL
1 tsp.	dry mustard	5 mL
1/2	onion, grated	1/2
	salt and pepper to taste	
1/2 tsp.	hot pepper sauce	2 mL
	chopped green onion for garnish (optional)	

1. Mash eggs with fork until crumbly. Stir in mayonnaise.
2. Add mustard, onion, salt, pepper and hot pepper sauce. Mix well. Serve on toast rounds or in sandwiches. Garnish with green onion, if desired.

Serves 4-6

Stuffed Eggs

Tabasco adds zest to these Devilled Eggs.

12	hard-boiled eggs	12
½ cup	mayonnaise	125 mL
½ tsp.	dry mustard	2 mL
1	small onion, minced	1
	salt and pepper to taste	
1 tsp.	Tabasco sauce	5 mL
	slivers of red pepper for garnish	

1. Cut eggs in half lengthwise. Remove yolks.
2. Mash yolks until crumbly. Add mayonnaise and remaining ingredients, except for red pepper.
3. Refill hollows of whites with yolk mixture. Decorate with slivers of red pepper.

Serves 12

Cheese Spread

A delicious spread for sandwiches. My mother also adds food colouring to some of the cheese spread to make decorative sandwiches.

2 cups	grated Cheddar cheese	500 mL
4 oz.	butter	115 g
1 tbsp.	milk	15 mL
1 tbsp.	prepared or Dijon mustard	15 mL
	salt and pepper to taste	
1 tsp.	hot pepper sauce (optional)	5 mL

1. Beat or blend cheese, butter and milk until smooth.
2. Add mustard, salt, pepper and pepper sauce.
3. Mix well.

Yields 1 cup (250 mL)

Cheese Straws

These spicy straws are wonderful with drinks.

6 oz.	butter	170 g
8 oz.	flour (1 cup [250 mL])	250 g
8 oz.	grated Cheddar cheese	250 g
½ tsp.	salt	2 mL
½ tsp.	pepper	2 mL
1 tsp.	dry mustard	2 mL
2	egg yolks, beaten	2
¼ cup	ice water	50 mL

1. Rub butter into flour or combine with a pastry blender. Add grated cheese, salt, pepper and mustard; mix thoroughly.
2. Add beaten egg yolks and ice water to make a stiff dough.
3. Roll out to about ¼" (1 cm) thick. Cut into strips 2½" x ½" (6 cm x 1.3 cm) for straws. These may be twisted into different shapes for variety.
4. Place straws on a baking sheet. Bake at 400°F (200°C) for about 15 minutes.

Makes about 30 straws

Hot Potato Balls

These are also known as Alu Balls, Alu is the Indian word for potato.

1 lb.	medium-sized potatoes	500 g
1	small onion, chopped finely	1
½ tsp.	garlic powder	2 mL
1 tsp.	cumin powder	5 mL
	salt and pepper to taste	
½ tsp.	chili powder (optional)	2 mL
¼ cup	flour	50 mL
	oil for deep-frying	

BATTER:

½ cup	dry ground yellow split peas	125 mL
½ tsp.	garlic powder	2 mL
½ tsp.	onion powder	2 mL
	salt and pepper to taste	
	water	

1. Boil potatoes in jackets. When skin splits, remove from heat and drain.
2. Peel off skin carefully. Crush pulp until texture is like a smooth pastry dough.
3. Add seasonings, mix thoroughly and shape into balls.
4. Combine all dry batter ingredients. Add just enough water to make batter a semisoft consistency, like thick cream.
5. Roll each ball in dry flour, then dip into prepared batter.
6. Heat oil to 365°F (185°C). Deep-fry balls in hot oil until golden brown.

Serve hot as an appetizer or a snack.

Makes 16-18 balls

Phulourie

This speciality was brought to the Caribbean by the East Indians and it is now enjoyed by all nationalities.

1 cup	dry, ground split peas	250 mL
	water	
1	small onion, finely chopped	1
2	garlic cloves, minced	2
½ tsp.	cumin powder	2 mL
	salt and pepper to taste	
½ tsp.	curry powder	2 mL
½ tsp.	hot pepper sauce	2 mL
	oil for deep frying	

1. Mix ground peas and just enough water to form a thick batter.
2. Add all ingredients and beat well, until light and fluffy.
3. Heat oil to 365°F (185°C).
4. Form the pea mixture, a tablespoonful (15 mL) at a time, into balls and drop into hot oil. Fry until golden brown, about 10 minutes.

Delicious served with mango chutney.

Makes 24

Did you know that about one million people of East Indian descent live in the English-speaking Caribbean alone?

Salt Fish Cakes

A West Indian favourite made with some variations in the different islands.

1 lb.	salt cod fish	500 g
1 lb.	potatoes, boiled and mashed	500 g
1	onion, chopped	1
	salt and pepper to taste	
½ tsp.	garlic powder	2 mL
¼ tsp.	dried thyme	1 mL
2	eggs, lightly beaten	2
½ cup	milk	125 mL
1 tbsp.	butter	15 mL
	bread crumbs	
	vegetable oil for pan frying	

1. In water to cover, boil cod fish for ½ hour. Drain off water, add fresh water and boil again for another ½ hour.
2. Remove skin and bones and discard; shred fish.
3. Add potatoes, onion, seasonings, 1 egg, milk and butter and mix well.
4. Form fish mixture into oblong cakes, about 4" (10 cm) long. Dip into beaten egg, then bread crumbs and pan fry in hot oil until golden brown. Drain well.

Serve hot as an appetizer or with a meal.

Makes 20-24.

Shrimp Cakes

Delicious with drinks or as a first course.

4 oz.	small peeled shrimp, canned OR fresh	115 g
1 tbsp.	butter	15 mL
1	small onion, chopped	1
½ tsp.	garlic powder	2 mL
¼ tsp.	paprika	1 mL
	salt and pepper to taste	
1 tsp.	hot pepper sauce (optional)	5 mL
1	egg, beaten	1
2 tsp.	butter OR margarine	10 mL
½ cup	milk	125 mL
½ cup	flour	125 mL
½ tsp.	baking soda	2 mL
	oil for deep-frying	

1. Pan fry shrimp in a hot pan, with butter, for a few minutes, just until pink.
2. Place shrimp in a bowl; add seasonings, beaten egg, butter, milk, flour and baking soda to make a thick batter.
3. Heat oil to 365F (185C). Scoop out batter with a tablespoon (15 mL), drop into hot oil and deep-fry. Drain on paper towels.

Serve with toast or crackers.

Serves 6.

The famous Pitch Lake in Southern Trinidad has been exploited since 1886 and the asphalt production has averaged 130,000 tons per year.

Crab Backs

Guyana

In the islands, land crabs are used for this dish because they are popular and readily available.

12	blue crabs	12
1	large onion, chopped	1
1	garlic clove, minced	1
2 tbsp.	cooking oil	30 mL
	salt and pepper to taste	
1 tbsp.	chopped green onion	15 mL
2 tsp.	lemon juice	10 mL
1 tsp.	hot pepper sauce	5 mL
4 tbsp.	bread crumbs	60 mL
2 tbsp.	butter	30 mL
	red pepper for garnish	
	parsley for garnish	

1. Clean and scrub crabs. Put crabs in cold water to cover. Bring to a boil. Boil for ½ an hour.
2. Cool crabs in cold water. Carefully remove backs from crabs and separate meat from claws and legs.
3. Clean shells (backs) thoroughly for filling.
4. Sauté onions and garlic in oil, add flaked crabmeat, salt and pepper. Stir-fry for 5 minutes.
5. Add green onions, lemon juice, pepper sauce, 2 tbsp. (30 mL) bread crumbs and 1 tbsp. (15 mL) butter. Mix well. Cool for 10 minutes.
6. Pile crab mixture into clean, empty crab shells. Sprinkle with bread crumbs and dot with butter.
7. Bake at 350°F (180°C) for 15-20 minutes. Garnish with slivers of red pepper and parsley sprigs before serving.

Serves 12.

Note: *If live crabs are unavailable use fresh, frozen or canned crab-meat. Substitute scallop shells for crab shells.*

See photograph on front cover.

Curried Meatballs

This delicious appetizer recipe was given to me by a friend from South Africa

1 lb.	minced round steak	500 g
1 cup	bread crumbs	250 mL
1	egg, beaten	1
2 tsp.	curry powder	10 mL
¾ tsp.	salt	3 mL
1	onion, chopped	1
1 tbsp.	chopped green onion	15 mL
2 tsp.	hot pepper sauce	10 mL

1. Combine all ingredients.
2. Shape into balls about 1" (2.5 cm) in diameter.
3. Bake in a lightly greased pan at 350°F (180°C) until brown on all sides, about 30 minutes.

Serve hot on cocktail picks.

Makes 24 meatballs

The Caribbean moon-lit night is an exotic experience to visitors. The brilliance of the moon, the reflections in the water and the silhouette of palms and tropical trees present a memorable picture.

Hot Pepper Sauce

Guyana

*Every island has its recipe for hot pepper sauce,
— with some variations Caribbean peppers are
hot and tasty*

1	small green papaw *	1
½ lb.	hot peppers, seeded and crushed	250 g
1	firm cucumber, chopped	1
2	onions, finely chopped	2
2	garlic cloves, minced	2
1 tbsp.	salt	15 mL
2 cups	vinegar	500 mL
1 tbsp.	prepared mustard	15 mL
1 tsp.	olive oil	5 mL

1. Boil seeded green papaw until tender; peel and chop coarsely.
2. Combine hot peppers with papaw, cucumber, onions, garlic, salt, vinegar, prepared mustard and olive oil. Simmer gently for 10 minutes. Cool. Store in jars.

Makes about 4 cups (1 L).

* Papaya is another name for papaw.

*Legend has it that the island of Tobago was the
home of Robinson Crusoe.*

Curry Powder

This recipe is a mixture of ground, dry spices brought to the Caribbean by the migrant workers from India.

6	cardamoms	6
8 oz.	coriander seed	55 g
2 oz.	cumin seed	55 g
1 tbsp.	mustard seed	15 mL
1 tbsp.	fenugreek seed	15 mL
2 oz.	black peppercorn	55 g
6	cloves	6
3 oz.	ground turmeric	75 g

1. Remove skins from cardamoms and discard
2. Toast coriander, cumin, mustard and fenugreek seeds in a heavy frying pan for about 5 minutes.
3. Grind in an electric blender, adding the peppercorn and cloves. Mix in ground turmeric.

Store in an air-tight jar.

Note: *Curry powder may also be bought commercially.*

Garam Masala

This spicy combination gives extra taste and fragrance to curried dishes.

10	large cardamoms	10
2 oz.	coriander seeds	55 g
2 oz.	black peppercorn	55 g
2 oz.	black caraway seed	55 g
2 oz.	fenugreek seed	55 g
2 oz.	mustard seed	55 g
2 oz.	cumin seed	55 g
8	cloves	8
½ oz.	ground cinnamon	15 g

1. Remove the skins from the cardamoms and discard.
2. Mix cardamom with coriander, peppercorns, caraway, fenugreek, mustard, cumin and cloves. Grind in an electric mill to a fine grain. Mix in ground cinnamon.
3. Store in an air-tight jar.

Note: *Ready-to-use Garam Masala may be bought in specialty stores.*

150 years ago the first ship sailed from India with labourers to work in the plantations of the Caribbean.

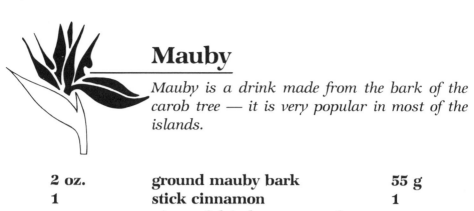

Mauby

Mauby is a drink made from the bark of the carob tree — it is very popular in most of the islands.

2 oz.	**ground mauby bark**	55 g
1	**stick cinnamon**	1
	piece of dried orange peel	
6	**cloves**	6
12	**cups water**	3 L
2 lbs.	**sugar**	1 kg

1. Boil mauby bark, cinnamon stick, orange peel and cloves in 1 cup (250 mL) of water for about 15 minutes. Cool. Strain.
2. Add the remaining water and stir in the sugar until dissolved. Brew for about 5 minutes, pouring from one container to another, until froth appears.
3. Fill bottles, leaving neck unfilled, for fermentation to occur. Cover and leave for 3 days. This drink is ready for use when the white foam comes above the neck of the bottle.

Serve cold.

Yields 4, 26 oz. (750 mL) bottles

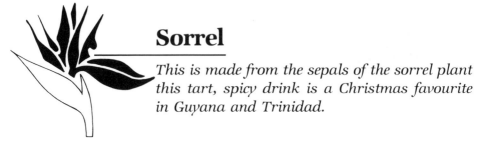

Sorrel

This is made from the sepals of the sorrel plant this tart, spicy drink is a Christmas favourite in Guyana and Trinidad.

4 cups	Sorrel sepals	1 L
6-8	cloves	6-8
	piece of orange peel	
8 cups	boiling water	2 L
	sugar to taste	
¼ cup	rum (optional)	50 mL

1. Remove the seeds from the sorrel; put into a jar with cloves and orange peel. Pour boiling water over sorrel. Cover jar and let stand for 24 hours.
2. Strain sorrel liquid. Sweeten to taste. Bottle and store in refrigerator.
3. If rum is used, add before bottling.

Serve cold.

Yields 2½ quarts (2.5 L).

* Dried sorrel may be substituted for fresh, use 2 oz. (60 g) dried sorrel in this recipe.

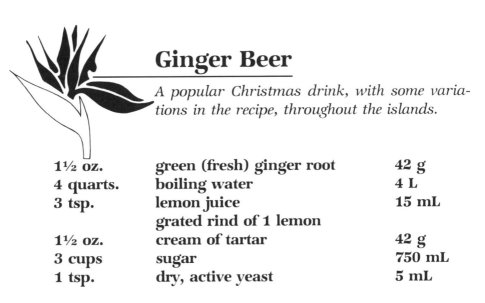

Ginger Beer

A popular Christmas drink, with some variations in the recipe, throughout the islands.

1½ oz.	green (fresh) ginger root	42 g
4 quarts.	boiling water	4 L
3 tsp.	lemon juice	15 mL
	grated rind of 1 lemon	
1½ oz.	cream of tartar	42 g
3 cups	sugar	750 mL
1 tsp.	dry, active yeast	5 mL

1. Pound the ginger root, combine with boiling water, lemon juice, lemon rind, cream of tartar and sugar stirring constantly.
2. When lukewarm, add dissolved yeast, stir and pour into a jar. Cover tightly and leave for 2 days.
3. Strain ginger liquid and bottle. Keep at room temperature for a further 3-4 days, store in a dark place to ripen. Chill before serving.

Yields 4 quarts (4 L).

Angostura bitters is probably the most widely known export of Trinidad. The company originally founded in Venezuela, later moved to Trinidad, bringing with it the "secret formula" for Angostura bitters.

Eggnog

A Christmas and New Year's favourite.

6	eggs, separated	6
¾ cup	sugar	175 mL
½ tsp.	vanilla essence (extract)	2 mL
¼ tsp.	nutmeg	1 mL
1 cup	rum	250 mL
1 cup	brandy	250 mL
2 cups	cold milk	500 mL
2 cups	whipping cream, whipped	500 mL

1. Beat egg yolks until thick and lemon coloured. Add ½ cup (125 mL) of sugar, vanilla and nutmeg, beating constantly.
2. Stir in rum and brandy; chill. Stir in milk when ready to serve.
3. Beat egg whites to form soft peaks, gradually add ¼ cup (50 mL) of sugar, beating until stiff peaks are formed.
4. Just before serving, fold in stiffly beaten egg whites and whipped cream.

Makes about 24 servings

Rum Punch

I make my punch from a formula from England, 1-sour, 2-sweet, 3-strong, 4-weak.

1 oz.	lime juice	30 g
2 oz.	prepared sugar syrup OR granulated sugar	55 g
3 oz.	rum of choice	85 g
4 oz.	iced water	115 g
	dash of Angostura bitters	
	lemon slice for garnish	

1. Combine lime juice, syrup, rum and water, stir well. Chill.
2. Pour into a tall glass, add a few drops of Angostura bitters and garnish with a lemon slice.

Serves 1

Planter's Punch

A favourite of all the islands. Recipe varies from island to island

1 cup	lime juice	250 mL
1 cup	prepared sugar syrup *	250 mL
12 oz.	vodka, whiskey or rum	340 g
	dash of Angostura bitters	
2 cups	crushed ice	500 mL
1	banana	1
1	orange	1
	mint sprigs	

1. Blend lime juice, syrup, rum, bitters and ice in a blender at medium speed until desired consistency is reached.
2. Serve in punch glasses and decorate with banana slices, orange pieces and a sprig of mint.

Serves 8-10

* To make a simple sugar syrup, combine 2 cups (500 mL) of sugar and 1 cup (250 mL) of water in a saucepan. Bring to a boil and boil for 5 minutes. Cool, refrigerate and use as needed.

Piña Colada

My favourite recipe from St. Lucia.

2 oz.	pineapple juice	60 mL
1 oz.	coconut cream	30 mL
2 oz.	rum, light	60 mL
1 cup	crushed ice	250 mL
	pineapple slice	
	maraschino cherry	

1. In a blender, blend pineapple juice, coconut cream, rum and ice for a few seconds, until creamy.
2. Pour into tall glass. Decorate with pineapple slice and cherry.

Serves 1

Banana Daiquiri

A frosty treat for any summer party!

2 oz.	light rum	60 mL
½ oz.	lime juice	15 mL
½ oz.	banana liqueur	15 mL
1	small banana, sliced	1
½ cup	crushed ice	125 mL

1. Blend rum, lime juice, liqueur and half banana with ice until smooth and frothy.
2. Pour into a martini or champagne glass and decorate with a banana slice.

Serves 1

Variations: *To make a* **Lime Daiquiri,** *omit banana liqueur and banana, add ½ oz. (15 mL) of Triple Sec and 1 tsp. (5 mL) fine (berry) sugar. For a* **strawberry, peach** *or other* **fruit daiquiri** *substitute fruit of your choice for banana and banana liqueur. For special occasions, rub lime wedge over rim of glass and dip rim into sugar.*

Peanut Punch

A popular drink in Trinidad

1 tbsp.	cornstarch	15 mL
¼ cup	water	50 mL
3 tbsp.	peanut butter	45 mL
1 cup	milk	250 mL
	sugar to taste	

1. Mix cornstarch in water; add peanut butter, milk and sugar. Heat until dissolved and well mixed.
2. Cool. Refrigerate. Serve over crushed ice.

Serves 1

Soups,
Salads
&
Vegetables

Chilled Cucumber Soup

Barbados

Very refreshing in the heat of the tropics

3 cups	peeled and shredded cucumbers	750 mL
1	small onion, finely chopped	1
5 cups	chicken stock (canned, homemade or cubes)	1.25 L
	salt and pepper to taste	
2 tsp.	cornstarch	10 mL
1 tbsp.	water	15 mL
1 cup	heavy cream	250 mL
1 tsp.	sherry	5 mL
2 tsp.	chopped parsley	10 mL
	cucumber slices	

1. Place cucumbers, onion and chicken stock into a saucepan; cover and simmer gently for 10-15 minutes.
2. Remove from heat, cool; place in blender and purée. Add salt and pepper.
3. Mix cornstarch with 1 tbsp. (15 mL) water. Stir into soup. Simmer until soup thickens, stirring constantly.
4. Remove from heat. Stir cream and sherry into soup.
5. Chill thoroughly. Mix well before serving. Garnish individual soup bowls with chopped parsley and translucent cucumber slices.

Serves 6

Avocado Soup

Easy to prepare, a smooth rich soup.

3	avocados, peeled, chopped	3
2 tbsp.	lime juice	30 mL
¼ tsp.	nutmeg	1 mL
	salt and pepper to taste	
½ tsp.	hot pepper sauce	2 mL
¼ cup	white rum (optional)	50 mL
6 cups	hot chicken stock	1.5 L
	yogurt for garnish	
	lime slices for garnish	

1. Place avocado pulp, lime juice, nutmeg, salt, pepper, hot pepper sauce and rum in blender.
2. Gradually add half of hot chicken stock and purée until smooth.
3. Stir remaining chicken stock into avocado purée and chill soup thoroughly.
4. Garnish individual servings with a spoonful of yogurt and a lime slice, if you wish.

Serves 8

Jamaica is one of the most beautiful islands in the Caribbean with beaches of white sand, facilitating every kind of water sport.

Frosted Raspberry Soup

Chilled fruit soups have become popular throughout the islands in recent years.

2 cups	fresh OR frozen raspberries	500 mL
½ cup	sugar	125 mL
2 tsp.	lemon juice	10 mL
½ cup	yogurt OR sour cream	125 mL
2 cups	cold water	500 mL
½ cup	red wine	125 mL
	yogurt for garnish	
	mint sprigs for garnish	

1. Purée raspberries with sugar, lemon juice and yogurt.
2. Stir in water and wine. Strain soup to remove raspberry seeds, if desired.
3. Chill thoroughly. Serve in frosted glass bowls or stemmed glasses and garnish each bowl with a spoonful of yogurt and a mint sprig.

Serves 4-6

Variations: *Substitute ripe papaya or mango pulp for raspberries and substitute white wine for red.*

Carnival, an annual event in Trinidad is a spectacle of colour and gaiety with costumes, parades, calypso, dancing in the streets and music by steel bands. It starts two days before Ash Wednesday and ends in the early hours of Ash Wednesday.

Split Pea Soup

An island soup that is also a treat on a cold, blustery day

1 cup	green or yellow split peas	250 mL
1	ham bone	1
6 cups	water	1.5 L
1	potato, grated	1
½ cup	diced carrots	125 mL
1	onion, chopped	1
1	garlic clove, minced	1
	salt and pepper to taste	
1 tsp.	hot pepper sauce (optional)	5 mL
	bunch of fresh mixed herbs *, tied with a string	

1. Boil the split peas with ham bone until tender, about 2½-3 hours. Remove bone and cut up meat.
2. Add potato, carrots, onions, garlic and seasonings; return meat to soup and simmer for 20 minutes. Remove herb bundle before serving.

Serve hot

Serves 4-6

* If fresh herbs are unavailable add ½ tsp. (2 mL) dried thyme, 2 or 3 sprigs of parsley, bay leaf and small celery stalk with leaves.

Black Bean Soup

Variations of this Caribbean favourite abound, from island to island and family to family.

2 cups	dried black beans	500 mL
1	pig's tail	1
1	onion, chopped	1
2	garlic cloves, minced	2
¼ cup	chopped green onion	50 mL
½ tsp.	dried thyme	2 mL
1	sprig of parsley	1
1	bay leaf	1
	salt and pepper to taste	
6 cups	chicken stock	1.5 L

1. Soak black beans in cold water overnight.
2. Drain beans, discard water and place black beans in a large saucepan.
3. Add remaining ingredients. Simmer until beans are tender, about 2-2½ hours.
4. Remove pig's tail, discard bay leaf and purée soup until smooth. Reheat.

Serve hot.

Serves 6

Variations: *If a pig's tail is not available, add 2 cups (500 mL) finely chopped lean ham or Spicy Spanish or Italian sausage to bean purée. You may also add finely chopped ripe tomato for colour and texture. If you like it hot, add hot pepper sauce or hot chili powder (cayenne) to taste. A dash of cinnamon also adds an interesting flavour note.*

Corn Soup

Guyana

Enjoy this rich combination of corn and chicken.

2 lbs.	chicken pieces	1 kg
1	onion, chopped	1
	salt and pepper to taste	
½ tsp.	sugar	2 mL
6 cups	water	1.5 L
1 tbsp.	cornstarch	15 mL
¼ cup	water	50 mL
1	egg	1
14 oz. can	cream-style corn	398 mL
¼ cup	chopped green onions	50 mL

1. Boil chicken with onions, salt, pepper and sugar in 6 cups (1.5 L) of water for 30 minutes. Remove chicken from stock and strip meat from bones.
2. Mix 1 tbsp. (15 mL) cornstarch with ¼ cup (50 mL) of water. Stir into stock to thicken.
3. Whip egg and stir into stock with chicken strips and cream-style corn. Simmer for 10 minutes. Add green onions.

Serves 6

Kaietur Falls, 741 feet high, best known tourist feature in Guyana can be reached from Georgetown, the capital, by local air-carriers.

Chicken Soup

With fresh bread or biscuits this soup makes a meal.

3 lbs.	chicken pieces	1.5 kg
1 tbsp.	vinegar	15 mL
1 tbsp.	butter OR margarine	15 mL
1	large onion, diced	1
1	garlic clove, minced	1
6 cups	water	1.5 L
¼ cup	barley	50 mL
1 lb.	potatoes, cut into large pieces	500 g
1 cup	sliced cabbage	250 mL
½ cup	diced carrots	125 mL
	salt and pepper to taste	
½ tsp	thyme	2 mL
1 tbsp.	chopped green onion	15 mL

1. Wipe the chicken with the vinegar.
2. Sauté chicken in butter with onion and garlic, until light brown.
3. Add water and barley, cover, simmer for 45 minutes.
4. Add potatoes, cabbage, carrots, salt, pepper and thyme. Cook, covered, over low heat for 20 minutes or until ingredients are tender. Add green onions and serve.

Serves 8

Wanton Soup

This soup was brought to the Caribbean by the Chinese immigrants. There are large Chinese communites in Guyana, Trinidad and Jamaica.

2 lbs.	chicken pieces	1 kg
1 oz.	green (fresh) ginger root	30 g
2 quarts	water	2 L
½ lb.	minced pork, cooked	250 g
½ cup	chopped, cooked shrimp	125 mL
	salt and pepper to taste	
½ tsp.	sugar	2 mL
½ cup	chopped green onions	125 mL
	finely chopped small onion	
½ tsp.	vet-sin	2 mL
24	wanton wrappers *	24
1 bundle	bokchoy, chopped	1

1. Boil chicken with green ginger in water for 30 minutes. Remove chicken from stock and strip meat from bones. Discard ginger.
2. Combine minced pork, shrimp, salt, pepper, sugar, ¼ cup (50 mL) each green onions and finely chopped onion, and vet-sin.
3. Place a teaspoonful of pork mixture on each wanton wrapper, fold wrapper and seal edges with water.
4. Drop folded wanton leaves into stock with chicken strips and remaining onions. Cook for 8-10 minutes.
5. When wanton leaves float on top of stock, add chopped bokchoy and green onions. Heat for 2 minutes.

Serves 4-6

* Wanton wrappers and vet-sin may be purchased at a Chinese grocery. Wanton is the Caribbean spelling.

Lobster Chowder

Jamaica

This recipe was given to me by one of my friends from Jamaica, where they use the famous rock or spiny lobster, also called langouste or langosta

2	slices streaky bacon, diced	2
1	large onion, chopped	1
1 lb.	lobster meat, fresh, frozen or canned	500 g
4	medium potatoes, diced	4
⅓ cup	diced carrots	75 mL
1	bay leaf	1
1 tbsp.	finely chopped parsley	15 mL
¼ cup	chopped green onions	50 mL
1 tbsp.	tomato paste	15 mL
14 oz.	can of tomatoes	398 mL
3 cups	water	750 mL
1 tbsp.	coconut cream *	15 mL
	salt and pepper to taste	
1 tbsp.	butter OR margarine	15 mL
¼ cup	wine	50 mL
	cooked crumbled crisp bacon for garnish	

1. Fry bacon until crisp; remove from pan.
2. Sauté onions in bacon fat until glossy, add lobster meat and sauté for about 5 minutes or until cooked. Reserve.
3. In a deep saucepan, combine potatoes, carrots, bay leaf, parsley, green onions, tomato paste, undrained tomatoes, water and coconut cream. Simmer gently for 20 minutes, until potato is cooked.
4. Stir in lobster meat, salt, pepper, butter and wine. Heat until piping hot. Garnish with crumbled crisp bacon.

Serves 6-8

* Packaged coconut cream is available at West Indian grocery stores.

Fish Soup

This soup is popular in all of the islands and each island has its own variation.

1 lb.	fish (whitefish or snapper)	500 g
1	onion, chopped	1
1 tbsp.	butter OR margarine	15 mL
1	garlic clove, crushed	1
	salt and pepper to taste	
1	hot red pepper, whole	1
½ tsp.	thyme	2 mL
6 cups	water	1.5 L
1 tbsp.	ketchup	15 mL
1 lb.	potatoes, sliced	500 g
1 tbsp.	lime juice	15 mL
¼ cup	chopped green onion	50 mL

1. Clean the fish. Remove scales. Cut fish into slices.
2. Sauté onions and garlic in butter, avoid browning. Add fish and all remaining ingredients, except lime juice and green onions. Simmer for 30 minutes.
3. Remove fish from stock; remove and discard the bones.
4. Coarsely crush potatoes in stock; return fish to the soup and reheat.
5. Before serving, stir in lime juice and sprinkle green onions over individual servings.

Serves 6

Christopher Columbus discovered the West Indies in 1492. Each island has its specialties and many dishes are popular in all of the islands.

37

Callaloo Soup

Trinidad & Barbados

This creole soup is famous in Trinidad and Barbados but also in other islands; Jamaica, Grenada, St. Lucia.

20	Callaloo leaves *	20
6 cups	chicken stock	1.5 L
¼ lb.	salt pork, cubed	125 g
¼ lb.	salt beef, cubed	125 g
1	onion, chopped	1
2	garlic cloves, minced	2
¼ tsp.	thyme	1 mL
3 tbsp.	coconut cream OR ½ cup (125 mL) coconut milk	45 mL
8	okras, sliced	8
½ lb.	crab meat, fresh, canned or frozen	250 g
	salt and pepper to taste	
1 tsp.	hot pepper sauce	5 mL
1 tbsp.	butter	15 mL

1. Wash callaloo leaves and chop coarsely. Place in a large saucepan with chicken stock, salt pork, salt beef, onion, garlic and thyme. Cook until meat is tender, about 45 minutes. Remove meat and reserve.
2. Add coconut cream and okras, simmer for 10 minutes. Swizzle (purée) thoroughly until smooth.
3. Return meat to pot. Add crab, salt, pepper, hot pepper sauce to taste, and butter. Simmer for a few minutes.

Serve hot with Foo-Foo, page 57.

Serves 6

* Callaloo leaves, dasheen leaves, spinach, Chinese spinach or Swiss chard may be used.

See photograph opposite page 32.

Pepper Pot Soup

This spicy soup is not to be confused with Pepper Pot stew from Guyana or Trinidad.

1 lb.	stewing beef, cubed	500 g
½ lb	salt pork, cubed	250 g
8 cups	water	2 L
1 lb.	callaloo OR spinach, chopped	500 g
1 lb.	kale OR Swiss chard, chopped	500 g
1	onion, chopped	1
1	garlic clove, chopped	1
1	hot pepper, chopped	1
½ lb.	yams	250 g
½ lb.	eddoes OR coco *	250 g
	salt and pepper to taste	
12	okras (ladies fingers), cut in rings	12
1 tbsp.	butter	15 mL
4 oz.	cooked shrimp	115 g
2 tbsp.	coconut cream	60 mL

1. Simmer the meats in 6 cups (1.5 L) of water in a large pot, covered, for 1 hour.
2. Boil the callaloo and Swiss chard in another pot, with 2 cups (500 mL) of water, until tender. Purée greens and liquid.
3. Add onion, garlic, hot pepper, yams, eddoes, salt and pepper to beef mixture.
4. Simmer until vegetables are tender and soup appears to be thickened.
5. Sauté okras in butter, until tender, about 5-10 minutes. Gently add the okras to the soup with shrimp and creamed coconut. Cook for 5 minutes.

Serves 6-8

* Eddoes or coco are also known as taro, a root vegetable.

Mettem Or Mettagee

Guyana

A favourite dish from Guyana. This can be used as an entire meal.

6 oz.	mixed meat (salt beef OR pig's tail)	170 g
1 tbsp.	butter OR margarine	15 mL
	water	
8 oz.	salt fish (dried cod)	250 g
1	small dry coconut	1
1 lb.	green plantains	500 g
¼ lb.	yam	125 g
½ lb.	cassava * page 41	250 g
	salt and pepper to taste	
½ tsp.	thyme	2 mL
1 tsp.	hot pepper sauce	5 mL
1	large onion, cut into rings	1
1 tsp.	sugar	5 mL
6	okras	6
	Dumplings (optional), page 41	
	Butter Sauce, page 41	

1. Cut up meat. In a large saucepan, fry meat lightly in butter; cover with water and simmer for 20 minutes.
2. Soak salt fish in warm water for about 15 minutes. Drain. Remove skin and bones. Discard. Squeeze fish dry.
3. Grate coconut, add 2 cups (500 mL) of warm water, squeeze well and strain off coconut milk.
4. Arrange peeled vegetables and seasonings in layers over the meat, with salt fish on top. Add coconut milk and cook, covered, until almost tender, about 30 minutes.
5. Place onions and okras on top of salt fish. Steam, covered, for 10 minutes. Add dumplings, if you wish, and steam for another 8 minutes. Remove meat, salt fish and okras, place in a flat dish and moisten with butter sauce, recipe follows.

Serves 8

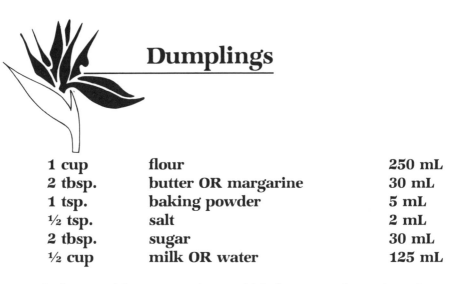

Dumplings

1 cup	flour	250 mL
2 tbsp.	butter OR margarine	30 mL
1 tsp.	baking powder	5 mL
½ tsp.	salt	2 mL
2 tbsp.	sugar	30 mL
½ cup	milk OR water	125 mL

1. Rub flour and butter together. Add baking powder, salt and sugar.
2. Mix with enough milk or water to make a stiff dough.
3. Form dough into balls and place on top of fish. Cook, covered, for 8 minutes. Do not open pot until dumplings are well risen.

Butter Sauce

1 tbsp.	butter OR margarine	15 mL
1	onion, chopped	1
1	tomato, diced	1
¼ cup	chopped green onions	50 mL
	soup stock	

1. Heat butter. Sauté onions, tomato and green onions until lightly browned.
2. Add 3-4 tbsp. (45-60 mL) of the liquid from the soup. Heat. Pour over meat, salt fish and okras. Serve with soup.

Note: *If dumplings are used, they should be added last.*

* Sweet cassava is a starchy root. When boiled it has a pleasant bland potato-like flavour. Grated cassava is made into a flat round bread that is popular throughout the islands.

Cabbage Soup

Originally, Portuguese traders brought this recipe to the islands during the seventeenth and eighteenth centuries.

1 lb.	stewing beef	500 g
2 oz.	salt beef, diced	55 g
2 oz.	salt pork, diced	55 g
8 cups	water	2 L
1 lb.	cabbage, finely sliced	500 g
3	potatoes, diced	3
1	turnip, diced	1
1	slice pumpkin, diced	1
1	large carrot, diced	1
1	large onion, diced	1
2	tomatoes, diced	2
	salt and pepper to taste	
2	garlic cloves, minced	2
½ tsp.	thyme	2 mL
2-3	sprigs parsley	2-3
1	bay leaf	1

1. Cut the meat into bite-sized pieces. Place in large saucepan, add water and bring to a boil. Cook for 35 minutes.
2. Add the sliced cabbage, simmer for 10 minutes, then add all the other diced vegetables, salt, pepper, garlic, thyme, parsley and bay leaf.
3. Simmer for about 1½ hours, until meat and vegetables are tender. If soup becomes too thick, boiling water may be added.

Serves 6-8

Lamb Soup

Beef, cow-heel, or oxtail may be substituted as alternative meat.

1½ lb.	lamb, neck or stewing meat	750 g
1 tbsp.	cooking oil	15 mL
1	large onion, chopped	1
2	garlic cloves, minced	2
8 cups	water	2 L
	salt and pepper to taste	
½ lb.	carrots, diced	250 g
1 lb.	mixed root vegetables, sliced *	500 g
	piece of hot pepper	
1 tbsp.	rice	15 mL
1	bay leaf	1
1 tbsp.	lime juice	15 mL
1 tsp.	chopped parsley	5 mL

1. Cut meat into small pieces.
2. Heat oil, sauté the onions and garlic until glossy. Add meat and fry for 10 minutes.
3. Add water, salt and pepper. Simmer for 1 hour.
4. Add carrots, root vegetables, hot pepper, rice and bay leaf. Cook until tender. Stir in lime juice and chopped parsley. Serve hot.

Serves 8

* Root vegetables consist of cassava, a tuberous root; taro, also known in Jamaica, Barbados, Trinidad and Guyana as coco, eddoe and baddo; yam, an edible tuber not to be confused with Louisiana yam.

Cucumber Yogurt

This can be served as a refreshing side dish with any curry.

1	medium-sized cucumber	1
1 cup	natural yogurt	250 mL
1 tsp.	crushed caraway seeds	5 mL
1 tsp.	garam masala	5 mL
1 tsp.	hot chili powder (cayenne)	5 mL
½ tsp.	sugar	2 mL
	salt to taste	

1. Peel cucumber, cut in quarters lengthwise, then slice thinly.
2. Combine yogurt with all the seasonings.
3. Add sliced cucumber. Mix well. Refrigerate for 1-2 hours. Serve cold.

Serves 3-4

Spicy Cucumbers

A cold tangy marinated salad

2	large cucumbers, peeled	2
1 tsp.	salt	5 mL
2 tsp.	minced hot peppers	10 mL
1	garlic clove, minced	1
1 tbsp.	lime juice	15 mL
	ground black pepper	

1. Cut cucumbers in half lengthwise and seed by scraping a small spoon down the centre. Slice crosswise.
2. In a bowl, salt cucumber slices, mix well, and let stand for ½ hour. Drain off liquid and gently squeeze cucumber slices.
3. In a serving bowl, combine cucumber, peppers, garlic and lime juice.
4. Marinate 1-2 hours or overnight. Sprinkle with black pepper before serving.

Serves 5-6

Julienne Of Vegetables

A colourful, make-ahead marinated salad.

4	large zucchini	4
4	medium carrots	4
1	medium green pepper	1
¼	medium head red cabbage	¼
¾ tsp.	salt	3 mL
¾ cup	mayonnaise	175 mL
1 tbsp.	prepared mustard	15 mL
1 tbsp.	minced parsley	15 mL
½ tsp.	dried tarragon	2 mL

1. Cut zucchini, carrots and green pepper into thin strips. Shred cabbage.
2. In a large bowl, toss zucchini, carrots and green pepper with ½ tsp. (2 mL) salt until well mixed.
3. In a medium-sized bowl toss red cabbage with ¼ tsp. (1 mL) of salt. Mix well. Cover both bowls and let stand for 1 hour.
4. Drain off liquid from both bowls.
5. In large bowl combine all the vegetables with mayonnaise, mustard, parsley and tarragon. Toss gently to coat with dressing. Cover and refrigerate for at least 1 hour.

Serves 6-8

Did you know that St. Vincent has the oldest Botanical Garden in the world?

Four Bean Salad

This salad has become popular across North America.

14 oz.	can cut green beans	398 mL
14 oz.	can cut yellow beans	398 mL
14 oz.	can red kidney beans	398 mL
14 oz.	can garbanzo beans	398 mL
½	white onion, thinly sliced	½
½	red onion, thinly sliced	½
1	green pepper, sliced	1
½ cup	salad oil	125 mL
¼ cup	vinegar	50 mL
1	garlic clove, minced	1
¼ tsp.	dry mustard	1 mL
½ tsp.	dried oregano leaves	2 mL
½ tsp.	dried basil leaves	2 mL

1. Drain cans of beans and combine with onions and green pepper.
2. In a bowl, whisk together dressing ingredients.
3. Pour over beans and stir well until coated.
4. Cover and refrigerate overnight.

Serves 6-8

Did you know that Christopher Columbus died in Spain in 1506, but his body was removed in 1536 to the Cathedral in Santo Domingo, the capital of the Dominican Republic?

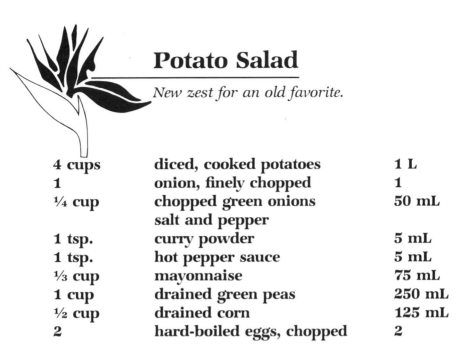

Potato Salad

New zest for an old favorite.

4 cups	diced, cooked potatoes	1 L
1	onion, finely chopped	1
¼ cup	chopped green onions	50 mL
	salt and pepper	
1 tsp.	curry powder	5 mL
1 tsp.	hot pepper sauce	5 mL
⅓ cup	mayonnaise	75 mL
1 cup	drained green peas	250 mL
½ cup	drained corn	125 mL
2	hard-boiled eggs, chopped	2

1. Combine potatoes, while still hot, with onions, green onions, salt, pepper, curry powder and hot pepper sauce. Let cool.
2. Blend mayonnaise into potato mixture. Add peas, corn and eggs, tossing lightly. Chill.

Serves 6-8

Barbados, discovered by ship-wrecked Portuguese sailors in 1536, is the most easterly of the West Indian Islands. In 1625 English Captain John Powell claimed the island for King James.

Fruit Salad

The Caribbean has an abundance of fruit of many varieties. Fruit is popular with everyone as snacks, in desserts and in salads.

½ cup	sugar	125 mL
1 cup	water	250 mL
1	banana	1
1	orange	1
1	grapefruit	1
1	papaya	1
12	cherries, preferably West Indian	12
2-3	slices of pineapple	2-3
1 tbsp.	sherry	15 mL

1. Boil sugar and water to form a thin sugar. Cool.
2. Peel banana, orange, grapefruit, papaya.
3. Cut fruits into small pieces. Pour the syrup over the fruit and mix. Chill several hours. Add sherry before serving.

Serves 4-6

Variations: *Substitute any fruit of your choice.*
— *For a* **Daiquiri Fruit Salad** *add 1 tsp. (5 mL) grated lime rind to warm sugar syrup. Cool. Add ¼ cup (50 mL) lime juice and ½ cup (125 mL) rum. Omit sherry. Chill several hours.*
— *For* **Minted Fruit Salad** *toss ½ cup (125 mL) finely chopped fresh mint leaves with fruit. Pour sugar syrup over and chill.*
— *For* **Gingered Fruit Salad** *add finely chopped fresh, preserved or crystallized ginger to sugar syrup. Adjust amount to your taste.*

Peppery Fruit And Vegetable Salad

Beautiful to look at with an intriguing flavour combination. Papaya seeds add peppery flavour.

2	ripe papayas, peeled, seeded, cubed (save seeds)	2
2	ripe avocados, peeled, cubed	2
1	cucumber, thinly sliced	1
1	purple onion, sliced in rings	1
2-3 quarts	mixed lettuce in bite-sized pieces	2-3 L
1½ cups	white wine vinegar	375 mL
1	onion, chopped	1
1	garlic clove, minced	1
1½ tsp.	salt	7 mL
½ tsp.	paprika	2 mL
1½ tsp.	dry mustard	7 mL
¾ cup	sugar	175 mL
3 cups	vegetable oil	750 mL
3 tbsp.	papaya seeds	45 mL

1. Combine fruit, vegetables and lettuce in a large bowl.
2. In a blender, thoroughly combine vinegar, onion, spices and sugar. Gradually blend in oil and then papaya seeds. Blend until seeds are coarsely chopped.
3. Toss salad with dressing and serve immediately. Refrigerate remaining dressing for later use.

Serves 12-14

Variation: *For a main course salad, add 2-3 cups (500-750 mL) cooked crab, shrimp, lobster or chicken.*

Chicken Salad

This is a popular dish in Guyana, usually served at parties.

4 cups	cooked, diced chicken	1 L
1 cup	chopped celery	250 mL
1 cup	cooked green peas	250 mL
1	small onion, grated	1
	salt and pepper to taste	
1	garlic clove, minced	1
2 tsp.	hot pepper sauce	10 mL
1 tsp.	paprika	5 mL
½ cup	mayonnaise	125 mL
2 tbsp	yogurt OR sour cream	30 mL
	lettuce	
	parsley for garnish	

1. Combine chicken, celery, green peas and onion in a bowl.
2. Add salt, pepper, garlic and pepper sauce. Mix well with mayonnaise and yogurt.
3. Chill thoroughly. Serve on a bed of lettuce and garnish with parsley.

Serves 6-8.

Salmon Salad

A light supper or lunch favourite.

5 oz.	can of salmon	142 g
1	celery stalk, diced	1
4	sour pickles, chopped	4
	salt and pepper to taste	
1 tbsp.	sugar	15 mL
1 tsp.	dry mustard	5 mL
1 tbsp	butter	15 mL
2 tbsp.	cream	30 mL
2 tbsp.	vinegar	30 mL
3	hard-boiled eggs, sliced	3
	lettuce leaves	

Salmon Salad

(Continued)

1. Combine salmon, diced celery, pickles, salt and pepper.
2. Stir sugar and mustard together in a small pot. Add butter, cream and vinegar. Cook until smooth. Cool.
3. Pour mustard dressing over salmon mixture and mix well. Decorate with hard-boiled eggs. Chill. Serve on crisp lettuce leaves.

Serves 3-4

Avocado And Tuna Salad

This can be served as a luncheon salad or a buffet dish.

1	ripe avocado	1
2	tomatoes, chopped	2
4 tbsp.	vegetable oil	60 mL
2 tbsp.	vinegar	30 mL
1	garlic clove, crushed	1
	salt and pepper to taste	
1 tsp.	sugar	5 mL
1 tsp.	hot pepper sauce	5 mL
6.5 oz.	can of tuna	184 g
1	small onion, finely chopped	1
¼ cup	chopped green onion	50 mL
	lettuce	

1. Peel, pit and chop the avocado. Add chopped tomatoes.
2. Combine oil, vinegar, garlic, salt, pepper, sugar and pepper sauce. Pour over avocado and tomato.
3. Break tuna into bite-sized pieces, add onions and green onion.
4. Combine tuna and tomato mixtures. Stir together until well mixed.
5. Refrigerate until cold. Serve on a bed of lettuce.

Serves 4-6

Lobster Salad

This is my favourite salad. It can be served as a meal or as an appetizer.

1 cup	cooked lobster meat	250 mL
2 tsp.	lemon juice	10 mL
2 tbsp.	mayonnaise	30 mL
	salt and pepper to taste	
1 tsp.	hot pepper sauce	5 mL
½ tsp.	paprika	2 mL
1	small onion, finely chopped	1
1	head lettuce	1
1	cucumber, sliced	1
	sweet pickle, sliced	
1	avocado, sliced	1

1. Flake lobster meat. Add lemon juice. Mix in mayonnaise, salt, pepper, hot pepper sauce, paprika and onion.
2. Arrange lobster mixture on a bed of lettuce and garnish with cucumber, sweet pickles and avocado. Chill before serving.

Serves 4-6

See photograph opposite page 48.

Reggae, a form of musical expression, originated in Jamaica. The best known interpreters of reggae music are Bob Marley, Peter Tosh and Max Romeo.

52

Curried Chana (Chick Peas)

Guyana & Trinidad

This is a favourite dish of the East Indian, vegetarian community.

19 oz.	can chick peas	540 mL
1	onion, chopped	1
1 tbsp.	cooking oil	15 mL
2 tsp.	curry powder	10 mL
1	garlic clove, minced	1
1 tbsp.	ketchup	15 mL
	salt and pepper to taste	
1 tsp.	hot pepper sauce	5 mL

1. Drain chick peas, retain ½ cup (125 mL) of liquid.
2. Sauté onion and garlic in oil. Add curry powder, cook gently for 1 minute.
3. Add chick peas to onion mixture, fry for about 5 minutes. Add remaining ingredients and reserved liquid. Simmer gently for about 15 minutes. Serve hot as a vegetable.

Serves 4

Did you know that 86% of Guyana's population is literate, education is compulsory between the ages of 5 to 14 and all education is free through to a University degree?

Dahl (Split Pea Purée)

Guyana & Trinidad

Dahl is the Hindu name for legumes or pulses. It is made with yellow split peas, brown lentils or small black beans split.

1 cup	dry yellow split peas	250 mL
4 cups	water	1 L
1 tsp.	curry powder	5 mL
1 tsp.	salt	5 mL
1	onion, finely chopped	1
1	small hot pepper, finely chopped	1
1 tbsp.	cooking oil or Ghee	15 mL
1	garlic clove, minced	1
1 tsp.	cumin powder	5 mL

1. Wash the peas, place in a large saucepan with water, add curry powder, salt, onion and hot pepper and boil for about 30 minutes. Turn heat low, simmer for 1 hour, until peas are tender.
2. Remove peas from heat, swizzle (purée) until mixture is smooth. Reheat.
3. In a small frying pan, heat oil, add garlic, sauté until brown; stir in cumin powder, sauté. Stir this mixture into peas and mix well.

Serve hot with boiled rice or roti, page 92.

Serves 4-6

Peas And Rice

Guyana

There are variations of this dish. In the Dominion Republic, red kidney beans are used with ham and bacon. In Jamaica, dry red peas or fresh pigeon peas are used with bacon.

1	small coconut	1
4-6 cups	water	1-1.5 L
¼ lb.	salt beef (optional)	125 g
1	onion, chopped	1
2 tbsp.	cooking oil	30 mL
1	garlic clove, minced	1
1 cup	peas (pigeon or black eye) *	250 mL
½ tsp.	thyme	2 mL
	salt and pepper to taste	
1 tsp.	lime juice	5 mL
1	hot pepper, chopped	1
2 cups	raw rice	500 mL
¼ lb.	dried shrimp (optional)	125 g

1. Grate coconut, add 2 cups (500 mL) of water. Let stand for 5 minutes. Squeeze coconut and extract liquid, which is called **coconut milk.**
2. Wash salt beef to remove excess salt; cut into small pieces.
3. In a large saucepan, sauté onion in oil until tender. Add salt beef and garlic, fry for about 15 minutes.
4. Add peas, cover with water by about 2" (5 cm). Cook, covered, until peas are tender, about 20 minutes.
5. Drain pea mixture and measure out 2 cups (500 mL) of liquid. Return liquid and peas to pot.
6. Add coconut milk, thyme, salt and hot pepper; liquid should measure 4 cups (1 L) before rice is added. Stir in rice.
7. Cover and cook gently over low heat for 15 minutes. Add shrimp, cook until rice is tender and all the liquid is absorbed.

Serves 6-8

* If fresh or canned peas are used, do not precook, simply add with rice.

Rice Pilau With Peas

This dish is popular with vegetarians and was brought to the Caribbean from India. Delicious with meat dishes.

2	onions, finely chopped	2
2 tbsp.	butter OR margarine	30 mL
½ tsp.	turmeric (optional)	2 mL
1 tsp.	garam masala	5 mL
4	cloves	4
2 cups	rice	500 mL
	salt and pepper to taste	
½ tsp.	chili powder (cayenne)	2 mL
4 cups	water	1 L
10 oz.	fresh, frozen or canned green peas	284 g

1. Sauté onion in butter until tender. Add turmeric, garam masala and cloves; fry on low heat for 1 minute.
2. Add washed, drained rice, salt, pepper and chili powder. Fry gently for a few mintues, stirring gently.
3. Add water and cook, covered, for 15 minutes. Add green peas; cook until rice is tender and liquid absorbed.

Serves 6-8

See photograph on back cover.

Foo-Foo

Pounded green plantains. Plantain is a member of the banana family and must be cooked before eating. This dish is served as a starchy vegetable. It is of African descent and is now found on all the islands.

3	green plantains	3
2 tbsp.	butter	30 mL
	salt to taste	

1. Peel plantains; boil in unsalted water until tender.
2. Chop plaintain coarsely, and pound in a large mortar. Dip pestle in cold water from time to time to prevent sticking. Plantain may also be processed in a food processor until smooth.
3. When smooth, mix with butter and salt. Form into balls and keep warm. Serve with soup.

Serves 6

Plantain Cakes

3	hard, yellow plantains	3
1 tsp.	salt	5 mL
2 tsp.	white pepper	10 mL
2 tbsp.	butter OR margarine	30 mL
1 tsp.	baking powder	5 mL
	oil for deep-frying	

1. Peel the plantains and cook in water until tender, about 30 minutes.
2. Chop plaintain coarsely, pound in mortar and mash until smooth or process in a food processor. Cool.
3. Add salt, pepper, butter and baking powder. Mix well. Shape into cakes about 1" (2.5 cm) in diameter.
4. Heat oil to 365°F (185°C). Deep-fry plantain cakes until light brown. Drain on paper towels.

Serve hot with fish or meat.

Serves 3-4

See photograph opposite page 64.

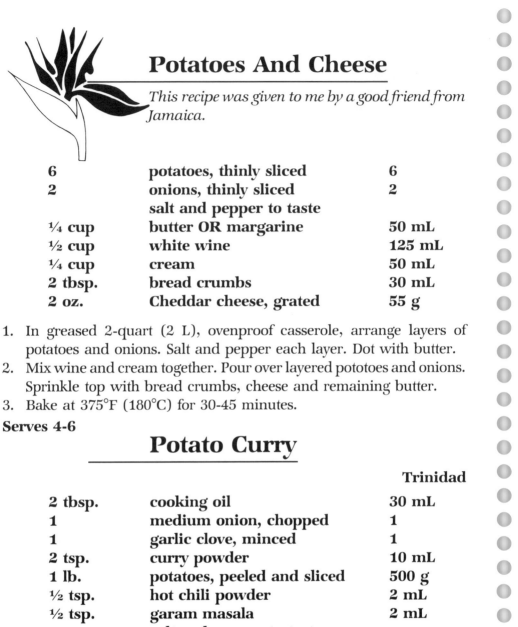

Potatoes And Cheese

This recipe was given to me by a good friend from Jamaica.

6	potatoes, thinly sliced	6
2	onions, thinly sliced	2
	salt and pepper to taste	
¼ cup	butter OR margarine	50 mL
½ cup	white wine	125 mL
¼ cup	cream	50 mL
2 tbsp.	bread crumbs	30 mL
2 oz.	Cheddar cheese, grated	55 g

1. In greased 2-quart (2 L), ovenproof casserole, arrange layers of potatoes and onions. Salt and pepper each layer. Dot with butter.
2. Mix wine and cream together. Pour over layered pototoes and onions. Sprinkle top with bread crumbs, cheese and remaining butter.
3. Bake at 375°F (180°C) for 30-45 minutes.

Serves 4-6

Potato Curry

Trinidad

2 tbsp.	cooking oil	30 mL
1	medium onion, chopped	1
1	garlic clove, minced	1
2 tsp.	curry powder	10 mL
1 lb.	potatoes, peeled and sliced	500 g
½ tsp.	hot chili powder	2 mL
½ tsp.	garam masala	2 mL
	salt and pepper to taste	
1 tbsp.	lemon juice	15 mL

1. Heat oil in frying pan. Sauté onion and garlic until tender. Add curry powder; fry for 2-3 minutes.
2. Add potatoes, chili powder, garam masala, salt and pepper. Mix well. Cook, covered, on low heat until potatoes are tender. You may need to add some water during cooking.
3. Add lemon juice before removing potatoes from heat. Stir. Finished dish should be dry. This is delicious with roti, page 92.

Serves 3-4

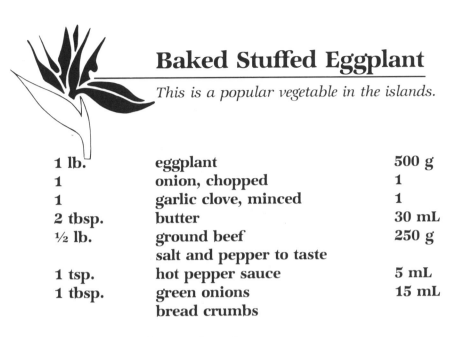

Baked Stuffed Eggplant

This is a popular vegetable in the islands.

1 lb.	eggplant	500 g
1	onion, chopped	1
1	garlic clove, minced	1
2 tbsp.	butter	30 mL
½ lb.	ground beef	250 g
	salt and pepper to taste	
1 tsp.	hot pepper sauce	5 mL
1 tbsp.	green onions	15 mL
	bread crumbs	

1. Boil eggplant in skin until tender.
2. Divide eggplant in half lengthwise. Carefully remove pulp, mash pulp until smooth. Retain skin.
3. Sauté onion and garlic in 1 tbsp. (15 mL) butter; add beef, salt, pepper and hot pepper sauce, fry for about 5 minutes. Add eggplant pulp and green onion. Mix well.
4. Return filling to skin. Sprinkle with bread crumbs and dot with butter.
5. Place in a greased baking dish and bake at 350°F (180°C) until brown, about 30 minutes.

Serves 6-8

Costries, the capital of St. Lucia has one of the safest harbours in the Caribbean and is a favourite port of call for cruise ships.

Cou-Cou (Coo-Coo)

Barbados

This cornmeal and okra cake is served with flying fish from Barbados.

4-6	okras, sliced in rings	4-6
2 cups	water	500 mL
1 tsp.	salt or to taste	5 mL
1 cup	cornmeal	250 mL
1 tbsp.	butter	15 mL

1. Boil okras in 1 cup (250 mL) of salted water until soft, 10 minutes.
2. Mix cornmeal with 1 cup (250 mL) of cold water. Pour the cornmeal mixture, in a slow stream, into the pot with okras. Stir ingredients with a wooden spatula over medium heat, beating all the time.
3. Cook until mixture is thick and smooth, about 5 minutes. Turn into a greased serving bowl or place on a warmed platter and spread liberally with butter. Serve warm.

Serves 4-6

Stuffed Mushrooms

Serve as an appetizer or vegetable.

1 lb.	medium mushrooms	500 g
1	small onion, grated	1
1 tbsp.	finely chopped green onion	15 mL
2	garlic cloves, finely chopped	2
¼ cup	butter OR margarine	50 mL
2 tbsp.	chopped parsley	30 mL
1 cup	bread crumbs	250 mL
½ cup	grated cheese	125 mL

1. Wash and dry mushrooms. Remove caps; chop stems finely.
2. Sauté onion, green onion and garlic in butter until soft. Add mushroom stems and parsley.
3. Stir in bread crumbs and cheese. Fill caps with onion mixture. Bake at 350°F (180°C) for 15 minutes.

Serves 6-8

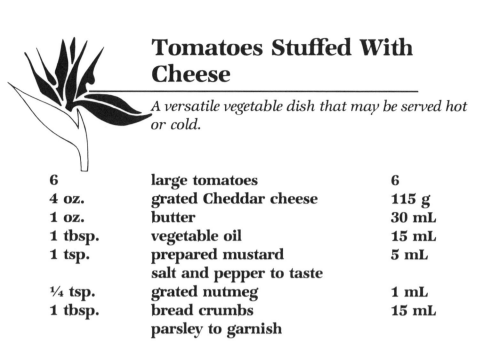

Tomatoes Stuffed With Cheese

A versatile vegetable dish that may be served hot or cold.

6	large tomatoes	6
4 oz.	grated Cheddar cheese	115 g
1 oz.	butter	30 mL
1 tbsp.	vegetable oil	15 mL
1 tsp.	prepared mustard	5 mL
	salt and pepper to taste	
¼ tsp.	grated nutmeg	1 mL
1 tbsp.	bread crumbs	15 mL
	parsley to garnish	

1. Cut tomatoes in half. Scoop out some of the seeds.
2. Combine grated cheese, butter, oil, mustard, salt, pepper, nutmeg and bread crumbs.
3. Place a scoop of cheese mixture in each tomato half.
4. Bake at 400°F (200°C) for 20-30 minutes. Garnish with parsley.

Serves 6-12

Variations: *Serve as an appetizer with buttered toast or with meat dishes. Step 4 may be omitted and tomatoes may be served cold on lettuce leaves.*

Lime Ginger Papaya

Serve this flavourful combination with seafood, chicken, pork or beef.

2	papayas, ripe but firm	2
4 tbsp.	butter	60 mL
2 tbsp.	lime juice	30 mL
2 tbsp.	rum OR brandy (optional)	30 mL
½ tsp.	ground ginger	2 mL
4	lime wedges	4
	hot pepper sauce	

1. Cut papayas in half, lengthwise, scoop out seeds. Pour ⅛" (0.5 cm) water in bottom of enamel or glass baking dish. Place papaya halves, hollow-side-up, in pan.
2. In papaya hollows, place 1 tbsp. (15 mL) butter, ½ tbsp. (7 mL) each lime juice and rum and ⅛ tsp. (0.5 mL) ground ginger.
3. Bake at 350°F (180°C) for 30 minutes, basting occasionally. Garnish with lime wedges. Add a dash of hot pepper sauce and serve warm.

Serves 4

Trinidad is the land of steel band, calypso and limbo. Oil drums are the major instrument of a typical steel band, while the limbo dancer attempts to "clear" under a bamboo bar as low as ten inches from the ground.

Fish,
Chicken,
Beef,
Lamb
&
Pork

Baked Stuffed Fish

A large whole fish is used for this recipe. Red snapper, queriman, salmon or similar fish may be used.

1	whole fish, 3-4 lbs. (1.5-2 kg), cleaned and scaled	1
3 tbsp.	butter OR margarine	45 mL
	salt and pepper to taste	
1	garlic clove, minced	1
1	large onion, thinly sliced	1
2 cups	bread crumbs	500 mL
¼ cup	green onions	50 mL
1	hot pepper, seeded and chopped	1
2 tbsp.	lime juice OR lemon juice	30 mL
1	tomato, sliced	1

1. Split the fish lengthwise to expose the cavity. Rub the fish inside and outside with a mixture of 1 tbsp. (15 mL) of butter, salt, pepper and garlic. Let stand while preparing stuffing.
2. In a small pan, heat 2 tbsp. (30 mL) butter, sauté half of the onions until soft, add bread crumbs, green onions, hot pepper, lime juice, salt and pepper, consistency of stuffing should be moist.
3. Fill cavity of fish with stuffing. Secure edges with skewers or sew together.
4. Place fish in a buttered baking dish. Arrange remaining onion slices and tomatoes over fish. Sprinkle with bread crumbs. Add 1 cup (250 mL) of hot water to dish. Bake at 400°F (200°C) for 30-40 minutes.

Serves 6

Variation: *Omit onion and tomato slices over fish if preferred. Baste with lime juice and garnish with lime wedges.*

See photograph opposite.

Ackee And Salt Fish

Jamaica

Ackee is the egg-shaped fruit of an evergreen tree grown in Jamaica; it has a scarlet shell, black seeds and cream-coloured flesh. The flavour is bland, like scrambled eggs.

24	ackees*, fresh or canned	24
½ lb.	salt fish (cod)	250 g
¼ lb.	salt pork, finely diced	125 g
2	medium onions, finely chopped	2
2 tbsp.	butter	30 mL
1	small hot pepper, chopped	1
3	green onion stalks, chopped	3
¼ tsp.	thyme	1 mL
4	tomatoes, finely chopped	4
6	bacon strips, fried crisp	6
½ tsp.	black pepper	2 mL

1. Remove all seeds, membranes, and red centres from ackees; boil for about 20 minutes. Drain and keep warm.
2. Wash salt fish, boil for about 25 minutes, until fish is tender. Pour off water; remove skin and bones, flake fish with a fork. Set aside in a warm dish.
3. Fry the diced pork until crisp and brown. Remove the pork. Sauté the onions in the fat until lightly brown; add butter, hot pepper, green onions, thyme and tomatoes. Fry for about 5 minutes.
4. Pour a small amount of fried onion mixture over the flaked fish, mix well. Add the ackees to fish, pour remaining onion mixture over the ackees; add diced pork. Lay crisply fried bacon on top. Sprinkle all with black pepper. Serve hot.

Serves 6

* If canned ackees are used omit Step 1.

Fried Salt Fish

Salt cod fish is popular in all Caribbean islands. Fish other than cod may be used.

½ lb.	dried salt fish	250 g
2 tbsp.	cooking oil	30 mL
1	medium onion, sliced	1
1	green pepper, sliced	1
½ tsp.	black pepper, sliced	2 mL
½ tsp.	garlic powder	2 mL
1 tsp.	hot pepper sauce	5 mL
1	medium tomato, chopped	1

1. Boil salt fish in water for 15 minutes. Remove skin and bones; squeeze fish dry. Flake fish.
2. Heat oil; sauté onion and green pepper, add fish and seasonings. Fry at medium heat.
3. Add tomatoes and fry until soft. Serve with bakes, page 96.

Serves 3-4

Fish In Beer

2 lbs.	fish of your choice	1 kg
2	garlic cloves, minced	2
¼ cup	chopped celery	50 mL
1 tbsp.	chopped parsley	15 mL
½ tsp.	thyme	2 mL
	salt and pepper to taste	
1 tsp.	hot pepper sauce	5 mL
2 tbsp.	lemon juice	30 mL
1 cup	beer	250 mL
2	bay leaves	2

1. Clean fish, cut in serving pieces. Arrange in a greased baking dish.
2. Season with garlic, celery, parsley, thyme, salt, pepper, hot pepper sauce and lemon juice. Let stand for 15 minutes.
3. Add beer and bay leaves. Cover with foil and bake at 350°F (180°C) for about 30 minutes.

Serves 6-8

Golden Grilled Red Snapper Steaks

Fish steaks, cutlets or fillets may be grilled. Any white fish may be used instead of red snapper.

4	red snapper cutlets	4
1 tbsp.	butter OR margarine	15 mL
2 oz.	Cheddar cheese, grated	55 g
2 tbsp.	ketchup	30 mL
	salt and pepper to taste	
½ tsp.	minced garlic OR garlic powder	2 mL
½ tsp.	paprika	2 mL
¼ tsp.	chili powder (cayenne)	1 mL

1. Place fish in a lightly greased ovenproof dish.
2. Combine butter and cheese with ketchup and seasonings.
3. Under a preheated grill, grill fish quickly for 2-3 minutes on 1 side.
4. Turn fish over, spread cheese mixture over the uncooked side. Return to grill.
5. Cook for 10 minutes; turn again and coat with remainder of cheese mixture. Grill until coating is brown and fish cooked thoroughly. Serve at once.

Serves 4

Bathsheba, an attractive resort on the Atlantic coast of the island of Barbados, is the home of the Flying Fish Fleet. Flying fish is one of the tastiest treats of Barbados.

Bajan Flying Fish

Barbados

"Bajan" is a shortened term for the word Barbadian. Flying fish are available in Barbados where large catches occur between December and June. They are often seen leaping in and out of the clear, warm waters of the Atlantic ocean. Delicious when boned, seasoned well and served steamed or fried.

6	boned flying fish *	6
2	limes	2
¾ tsp.	salt	3 mL
1	onion, chopped	1
¼ cup	chopped green onions	50 mL
2	garlic cloves, minced	2
½	hot pepper, chopped	½
½ tsp.	ground thyme	2 mL
¼ tsp.	ground cloves	1 mL
¼ tsp.	black pepper	1 mL
2 tbsp.	butter	30 mL
	bread crumbs	

1. Marinate fish with juice of 1 lime and ¼ tsp. (1 mL) salt for about 20 minutes.
2. Combine onion, green onions, garlic, hot pepper, thyme, cloves, ¼ tsp. (1 mL) salt and juice of 1 lime.
3. Wash fish and place in bowl; sprinkle fish with ¼ tsp. (1 mL) black pepper and ¼ tsp. (1 mL) salt. Spread onion mixture in grooves left after boning of fish or over fish fillets.
4. Melt butter in saucepan, dip fish in bread crumbs and fry in hot butter until brown, about 5-10 minutes. Serve with lime slices.

Serves 6

* Flying fish fillets may be used.

Curried Hassars

This fish is known as Hassar in Guyana and Cascadura in Trinidad. It is covered with a hard shell and lives in the swamps of the rice fields.

12	large hassars	12
3 tbsp.	salt	45 mL
3 tbsp.	sugar	45 mL
3	limes	3
3 tbsp.	vegetable oil	45 mL
1	large onion, chopped	1
3	garlic cloves, minced	3
3 tbsp.	curry powder	45 mL
	salt to taste	
¼ tsp.	black pepper	1 mL
½	hot pepper, chopped	½
½ cup	coconut milk * OR 2 tbsp. (30 mL) creamed coconut and ½ cup (125 mL) water	125 mL
2 cups	water	500 mL
¼ cup	chopped green onions	60 mL

1. Wash fish well to remove mud. Cut fish down the centre to expose cavity. Marinate with salt, sugar and the juice of 2 limes for about 1 hour.
2. Wash fish well in warm water, several times, to remove marinade. Squeeze dry.
3. Heat oil, sauté onions and garlic until tender. Add curry powder. Mix well. Add prepared hassars, salt and pepper to taste and hot pepper. Fry for about 5-10 minutes.
4. Add coconut milk and 2 cups (500 mL) of water or creamed coconut with 2½ cups (625 mL) cups of water. Add green onions and juice of 1 lime. Serve hot with boiled rice.

Serves 12

* For preparation of coconut milk, see page 55.

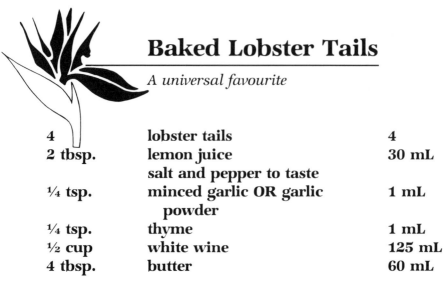

Baked Lobster Tails

A universal favourite

4	lobster tails	4
2 tbsp.	lemon juice	30 mL
	salt and pepper to taste	
¼ tsp.	minced garlic OR garlic powder	1 mL
¼ tsp.	thyme	1 mL
½ cup	white wine	125 mL
4 tbsp.	butter	60 mL

1. Soak lobster tails with 1 tbsp. (15 mL) of lemon juice in cold water for about 1 hour.
2. To prepare tails, make a slit down the upper surface of shell, pull tail out, place on top of shell with end still attached.
3. Mix the seasonings with white wine and pour over lobster tails. Dot with butter and bake at 375°F (190°C) for 25-30 minutes. Serve with hot butter and lemon juice.

Serves 4

Shrimp In Tomato Sauce

A colourful dish with an enticing aroma.

1	large onion, chopped	1
2	garlic cloves, minced	2
3 tbsp.	butter OR margarine	45 mL
1 cup	shelled and deveined shrimp	250 mL
	salt and pepper to taste	
½	green pepper, chopped	½
½ tsp.	paprika	2 mL
½ tsp.	chili powder	2 mL
1	medium tomato, chopped	1
2 tbsp.	tomato purée	30 mL
¾ cup	boiled rice	175 mL
2 tsp.	chopped parsley	10 mL

Shrimp In Tomato Sauce

(Contintued)

1. Sauté onions and garlic in butter until tender. Add shrimp, salt, pepper, green pepper, paprika, chili powder, tomato and tomato purée. Simmer for 15 minutes.
2. Serve over cooked rice. Garnish with parsley. Serve hot.

Serves 4-6

Curried Shrimp Or Prawns

Trinidad & Guyana

A delicious zesty dish that is easy to prepare.

2	onions, chopped	2
3	garlic cloves, minced	3
3 tbsp.	vegetable oil	45 mL
2 tbsp.	curry powder	30 mL
2 lbs.	raw, peeled shrimp	1 kg
	salt and pepper to taste	
1 tsp.	hot pepper sauce	5 mL
1	large tomato, chopped	1
2 tbsp.	butter	30 mL
2 tsp.	lemon juice	10 mL

1. Sauté onions and garlic in oil until tender, add curry powder, stirring for about 2 minutes.
2. Add shrimp, salt, pepper, hot pepper and tomatoes. Cook, uncovered, until shrimp is firm and pink, about 15 minutes. Add butter and lemon juice. Mix well.

Serve with hot, boiled rice or roti, page 92.

Serves 4-6

Cha Che Kai Chicken

Guyana

This popular dish is served as a main course or as an appetizer.

2 tsp.	ground ginger	10 mL
2	garlic cloves, minced	2
1	large onion, grated	1
2 tbsp.	soy sauce	30 mL
	salt and pepper to taste	
½ tsp.	paprika	2 mL
½ tsp.	vet-sin	2 mL
2 lbs.	chicken cut in serving-size pieces	1 kg
2	eggs, beaten	2
½ cup	flour	125 mL
	oil for frying	

1. Combine ginger, garlic, onion, soy sauce and seasonings to make a marinade.
2. Marinate chicken overnight in refrigerator.
3. Roll chicken pieces in beaten egg and then dip in flour.
4. Heat oil to 365°F (185°F), add chicken and fry until golden brown, about 20 minutes.

Serves 4-6.

The coastal strip of Guyana, the scene of agricultural and industrial activity, lies below sea level and is protected from high tides by sea-walls, dykes and drainage systems.

Chicken Curry

This dish is influenced by the East Indian population in Guyana, Trinidad and Jamaica with some variations, depending on the cook.

3 lbs.	chicken	1.5 kg
2 tbsp.	vegetable oil	30 mL
1	large onion, chopped	1
3	garlic cloves, minced	3
2 tbsp.	curry powder	30 mL
	salt and pepper to taste	
1 tsp.	hot chili powder (cayenne)	5 mL
1 tsp.	paprika	5 mL
2 cups	water	500 mL

1. Cut chicken into serving pieces.
2. In hot oil, sauté onions and garlic until tender, add curry powder, cook gently for 1-2 minutes.
3. Add chicken pieces, salt, pepper, chili powder and paprika; fry on medium heat for 10-15 minutes.
4. Add 2 cups (500 mL) of water, bring to a boil, then simmer, covered, for about 20 minutes or until chicken is tender.

Serve with hot boiled rice or with Dahl Puri, page 93.

Serves 6

See photograph on back cover.

Did you know that Barbados is one of the most densely populated places in the world, 1500 inhabitants to the square mile (600 to the square km)?

Chicken Pelau

Trinidad

This popular dish has some variations in the other islands. Beef or pork may be substituted for chicken.

3 lbs.	chicken, cut up	1.5 kg
	salt and pepper to taste	
1 tbsp.	curry powder	15 mL
2	garlic cloves, minced	2
¼ tsp.	fresh thyme	1 mL
1	hot pepper, seeded and minced	1
3 tbsp.	vegetable oil	45 mL
1	onion, chopped	1
4 cups	water	1 L
2 cups	long-grain rice, washed	500 mL
1 tbsp.	butter	15 mL
¼ cup	chopped green onions	50 mL

1. Season chicken with salt, pepper, curry powder, garlic, thyme and hot pepper. Let stand for 2-3 hours.
2. Heat oil; sauté onions and chicken until golden brown, add marinade and enough water to cover chicken pieces. Simmer gently for 30 minutes.
3. Strain the stock, measure; add enough water to make 4 cups (1 L). Return to chicken pieces; stir in rice, cover and simmer until rice is cooked, about 20 minutes. Add butter and green onions. Serve hot.

Serves 6-8.

Chicken Chop Suey

This exotic dish is from our Oriental heritage. There are large communities of Chinese in Jamaica, Trinidad and Guyana.

	piece of green (fresh) ginger, finely chopped	
2	garlic cloves, finely minced	2
	salt to taste	
1 tsp.	sugar	5 mL
1 tbsp.	shee-yow	15 mL
1 tbsp.	oyster sauce	15 mL
2 tbsp.	cooking wine	30 mL
3 tbsp.	vegetable oil	45 mL
2 lbs.	chicken, cut into small pieces	1 kg
¼ lb.	foo-chuk *	125 g
8 oz.	can bamboo shoots, drained	227 g
2 oz.	dried Chinese mushrooms	55 g
½ cup	water	125 mL
¼ cup	chopped green onions	50 mL
¼ cup	grated carrots	50 mL

1. Combine green ginger, garlic, salt, sugar, pepper, shee-yow, oyster sauce and cooking wine. Pour over chicken and marinate for 30 minutes.
2. Fry chicken, with marinade, in oil for 5 minutes; add foo-chuk, bamboo shoots and Chinese mushrooms. Add ½ cup (125 mL) water. Simmer on low heat for about 15-20 minutes. When completed, add green onions and grated carrots.

Serves 6

* Foo-chuk is a bean curd available at Chinese groceries.

Sweet And Sour Chicken

Guyana

This dish came from our Chinese comunity.

1	small onion, grated	1
1	garlic clove, minced	1
1 tbsp.	soy sauce	15 mL
2 tsp.	vinegar	10 mL
1 tsp.	celery powder	5 mL
1 tsp.	hot pepper sauce	5 mL
	salt and pepper to taste	
2 lbs.	chicken breast, cubed	1 kg
¼ cup	flour	50 mL
	oil for deep-frying	

1. Combine all ingredients, except chicken, flour and oil, to make a marinade. Add chicken. Marinate overnight in refrigerator.
2. Remove chicken pieces from marinade, flour lightly and deep-fry in 365°F (185°C) oil, until brown.

SAUCE:

1 tbsp.	Demerara sugar	15 mL
4 tbsp.	vinegar	50 mL
1 tbsp.	soy sauce	15 mL
2 tbsp.	ketchup	30 mL
2 tsp.	vet-sin	10 mL
	salt and pepper to taste	
½ cup	water	125 mL
2 tsp.	cornstarch	10 mL
¼ cup	water	50 mL
3 tbsp.	chopped, Chinese pickles	45 mL
1 tsp.	Chinese spice	5 mL
1	small onion, chopped	1

Sweet And Sour Chicken

(Continued)

1. Boil sugar with vinegar, soy sauce, ketchup, vet-sin, salt, pepper and water for about 1-2 minutes.
2. Dissolve cornstarch in water, add to sugar mixture. Stir and boil for 2 minutes. Add chopped pickle, Chinese spice and onion. Heat.
3. Pour sauce over chicken in ovenproof baking dish and bake for about 30 minutes. Serve with boiled rice.

Serves 4-6

Chicken Chow Mein

A Chinese favourite enjoyed by all nationalities.

2 lb.	chicken breast	1 kg
1 tbsp.	shee-yow *	15 mL
1 tsp.	Chinese spice	5 mL
	salt and pepper to taste	
1 tsp.	sugar	5 mL
1 lb.	egg noodles	500 g
½ lb.	mixed vegetables	250 g
2	bacon strips	2
1	onion, chopped	1
1	garlic clove, minced	1
1 tbsp.	butter OR margarine	15 mL
¼ cup	chopped green onions	50 mL

1. Boil chicken for about 10 minutes. Remove chicken strips and season with shee-yow, Chinese spice, salt, pepper and sugar.
2. Boil noodles in salted water for 5-7 minutes. Strain. Run cold water over noodles. Drain; set aside.
3. Cut bacon strips into small pieces, fry. Add onions, garlic, and mixed vegetables, stir-fry until tender. Add chicken strips, butter and noodles. Stir-fry for 5-7 minutes. Decorate with chopped green onions.

Serves 4-6.
  * Shee-yow is available at Chinese grocery stores.
 ** mixed vegetables may include sliced celery, carrots, mushrooms, broccoli florets, pea pods, etc.

Spicy Roast Chicken

A tangy dish with East Indian influences.

1 cup	natural yogurt	250 mL
3	garlic cloves, crushed	3
2 tsp.	grated green (fresh) ginger	10 mL
⅓ cup	lime juice	75 mL
1 tbsp.	ground coriander seed	15 mL
1 tsp.	ground cumin seed	5 mL
1 tsp.	hot chili powder (cayenne)	5 mL
	salt and pepper to taste	
3 lbs.	roasting chicken	1.5 kg
1	onion, sliced and steamed	1
1	lime, sliced	1

1. Mix yogurt, garlic, ginger, lime juice, spices, salt and pepper.
2. Rub chicken inside and outside with yogurt marinade mixture. Cover and leave overnight in refrigerator.
3. Remove chicken from marinade and roast in a preheated oven at 350°F (180°C) for about 1-1½ hours. Baste with marinade during cooking. Serve with steamed onion slices and lime.

Serves 4-6

Chicken In The Oven

1	onion, grated	1
2	garlic cloves, minced	2
2 tsp.	garam masala, page 20	10 ml
1 tbsp.	butter OR margarine	15 mL
2 tbsp.	tomato paste	30 mL
2 tbsp.	vinegar	30 mL
1 tsp.	hot pepper sauce	5 mL
	salt and pepper to taste	
3 lbs.	chicken pieces	1.5 kg

1. Combine all ingredients, except chicken, to make a marinade. Add chicken, toss well and let stand for 3 hours.
2. Bake chicken in marinade at 350°F (190°C) for 1 hour, until cooked.

Serves 6

Roast Chicken Or Turkey With Bread Stuffing

A traditional dish with a hint of spice.

4 lb.	roasting chicken	2 kg
1 tbsp.	vinegar	15 mL
	salt and pepper to taste	
1 tsp.	paprika	5 mL
1 tsp.	hot chili powder (cayenne)	5 mL
1 tsp.	minced garlic OR garlic powder	5 mL
3 tbsp.	butter OR margarine	45 mL
1	large onion, finely chopped	1
½ cup	chopped giblets	125 mL
2 cups	bread crumbs	500 mL
1 cup	mashed potatoes	250 mL
½ cup	water	125 mL

1. Wash chicken thoroughly inside and out. Dry.
2. Rub body cavity with a mixture of vinegar, half the seasonings and 1 tbsp. (15 mL) butter. Set aside.
3. To make stuffing, sauté onions in butter until tender. Add giblets and remaining seasonings. Fry for about 5-10 minutes. Remove from heat, combine with bread crumbs and mashed potatoes. Mix thoroughly. Cool.
4. Pile stuffing lightly into body cavity and neck of bird. Close openings with skewers. Place bird, breast upwards, on a rack in roaster. Cover loosely with a tent of foil. Add water to roaster. Roast for 20 minutes per lb. (40 minutes per kg), plus 20 minutes, at 350°F (180°C).
5. Uncover bird for last 30 minutes of cooking time to brown evenly. Baste with pan drippings.

Serves 6-8

Barbecued Chicken

This is popular at open-air parties and home parties. It provides an escape from the heat of cooking indoors.

3 lbs.	chicken (thighs and drumsticks)	1.5 kg
1	onion, grated	1
2	garlic cloves, minced	2
	salt and pepper to taste	
1 tsp.	hot pepper sauce	5 mL
½ tsp.	allspice	2 mL
½ tsp.	ground ginger	2 mL
¼ cup	vinegar	50 mL
¼ cup	lemon juice	50 mL
12 oz.	ketchup	340 g
4 tbsp.	sugar	60 mL
1 tbsp.	Worcestershire sauce	15 mL
½ tsp.	barbecue spice	2 mL

1. Wash and trim fat from chicken. Marinate chicken with onion, garlic, salt, pepper, allspice and ¼ tsp. (1 mL) ginger for about 2 hours.
2. Prepare barbecue sauce. Combine vinegar, lemon juice, ketchup, sugar, Worcestershire sauce, barbecue spice and ¼ tsp. (1 mL) ginger with juice from marinade. Simmer for 10 minutes, then cool.
3. Cook chicken over charcoal for about 20 minutes on each side. Baste meat with sauce. Cook at low heat. Turn, baste the other side and continue cooking.

Serves 6-8

Beef Stew

This savoury stew was introduced to Guyana by the West Africans.

2 tbsp.	vegetable oil	30 ml
1 tbsp.	brown sugar	15 mL
2	large onions, chopped	2
2	garlic cloves, minced	2
2 lbs.	stewing beef, cubed	1 kg
1	large tomato, chopped	1
	salt and pepper to taste	
½ tsp.	ground cinnamon	2 mL
1 tsp.	hot pepper sauce	5 mL
2½ cups	water	625 mL
2	carrots, peeled and sliced	2
¼ cup	chopped green onions	50 mL
1 tbsp.	cornstarch	15 mL
2 tbsp.	water	30 mL

1. Heat oil, add brown sugar; stir until sugar is melted and darkened.
2. Add onions and garlic, sauté until tender, then add meat, tomato, salt, pepper, cinnamon and hot pepper sauce. Brown for about 10 minutes, stirring continuously.
3. Add water and simmer, covered, until meat is tender, about 1 hour; then add carrots and green onions, simmer for 15 minutes.
4. Mix cornstarch with 2 tbsp. (30 mL) water to a smooth paste, add to stew. Stir constantly until stew is thickened, about 5 minutes. Serve with rice or noodles.

Serves 4-6

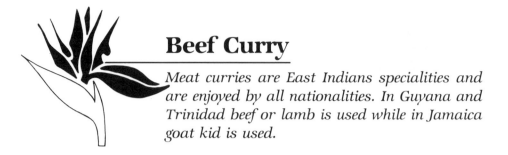

Beef Curry

Meat curries are East Indians specialities and are enjoyed by all nationalities. In Guyana and Trinidad beef or lamb is used while in Jamaica goat kid is used.

3 lbs.	beef, lamb or goat	1.5 kg
2 tbsp.	vegetable oil	30 mL
2	onions, finely chopped	2
3	garlic cloves, minced	3
3 tbsp.	curry powder	45 mL
	salt and pepper to taste	
1	hot pepper, chopped	1
1 tsp.	finely chopped green (fresh) ginger (optional)	5 mL
½ tsp.	allspice	2 mL
2 cups	water OR 1 cup (250 mL) coconut milk, page 55, and 1 cup (250 mL) water	500 mL

1. Remove fat from meat and cut into small serving pieces.
2. In hot oil, sauté onions and garlic until tender. Add curry powder, stirring for a few minutes. Add the meat, salt, pepper, hot pepper, green ginger and allspice; fry for about 10 minutes.
3. Add water or coconut milk, cook, covered, at a gentle simmer for about 2 hours or until meat is tender. Serve hot with rice or roti, page 92.

Serves 6.

Beef Olives

This recipe was given to me by a friend from England.

1 lb.	sirloin steak OR fillet	500 g
1 tbsp.	butter OR margarine	15 mL
½ cup	bread crumbs	125 mL
1 tbsp.	parsley	15 mL
1 tsp.	thyme	5 mL
	salt and pepper to taste	
1	egg, beaten	1
1 cup	beef broth	250 mL

1. Cut steak into thin slices 4" (10 cm) long and 2" (5 cm) wide.
2. Combine butter with bread crumbs, parsley, thyme, salt, pepper and eggs.
3. Spread a little of the butter mixture on each slice of beef, roll and tie with a piece of strong thread.
4. Bring the beef broth to a boil; add the olives and simmer gently for 1 hour. Remove the thread and serve with mashed potatoes.

Serves 4

Antigua, one of the first islands to be visited by sun-seekers, has on its southern coast English Harbour and Nelson's Dockyard. From this base Lord Nelson sailed against England's enemies in the Caribbean.

Stuffed Steak

This recipe is a culinary adoption from North America.

2 lbs.	sirloin steak	1 kg
4 oz.	oysters	115 g
2 tbsp.	bread crumbs	30 mL
2 tsp.	lemon juice	10 mL
½ tsp.	cayenne pepper	2 mL
	salt and pepper to taste	
1 tbsp.	olive oil	15 mL
4 oz.	chopped mushrooms	115 g
1	medium onion, chopped	1
1 tbsp.	butter	15 mL

1. Trim steak, remove any fat. Make a pocket in the meat with a sharp knife.
2. Chop the oysters finely, mix with bread crumbs, lemon juice, cayenne pepper, salt and black pepper.
3. Fill the pocket with the oyster mixture; rub steak with the olive oil.
4. Place steak in a hot frying pan with some butter and cook to required degree of doneness.
5. Sauté mushrooms and onions in butter. Put steak on a warmed serving platter, pour mushrooms and onions over it. Slice steak in thin diagonal slices, across the grain. Serve hot.

Serves 4-6.

Meat Sauce

This tasty recipe was given to me by a friend from Jamaica. Spaghetti sauces have become world favourites, even in the Caribbean.

3	medium onions, chopped	3
3	garlic cloves, crushed	3
3	green peppers, chopped	3
1 tbsp.	vegetable oil	15 mL
3 lbs.	ground lean beef	1.5 kg
2 x 14 oz.	cans plum tomatoes	2 x 398 mL
19 oz.	can regular tomatoes	540 mL
19 oz.	can stewed tomatoes	540 mL
5½ oz.	can tomato paste	156 mL
2 x 10 oz.	cans mushroom pieces	2 x 284 mL
	salt and pepper to taste	
1 tsp.	turmeric	5 mL
1 tsp.	sugar	5 mL
2 tsp.	hot chili powder (cayenne)	10 mL
	few basil leaves	
1 tsp.	oregano	5 mL

1. Sauté onions, garlic and green pepper in oil until tender. Add meat and brown lightly.
2. Add remaining ingredients, simmer covered for about 3-4 hours. Serve with spaghetti or rice.

Serves 6-8

Irish Stew

Since Britian had a powerful influence in the Caribbean and Guyana, many excellent recipes have been adopted by the island community of mixed peoples.

2 lbs.	lamb, cubed	1 kg
2	onions, chopped	2
2 tbsp.	vegetable oil	30 mL
	salt and pepper to taste	
½ tsp.	dried thyme	2 mL
1	garlic clove, minced	1
1	bay leaf	1
3 cups	water	750 mL
½ lb.	carrots, sliced	250 g
1 lb.	potatoes, sliced	500 g
½ lb.	small white onions, sliced	250 g
¼ cup	chopped green onions	50 mL
1 tsp.	chopped parsley	5 mL

1. Sauté lamb and chopped onions in heated oil. Add salt, pepper, thyme, garlic and bay leaf; cook slowly for 30 minutes.
2. Add water, carrots, potatoes and white onions. Simmer, covered, for about 1 hour or until meat is tender. Stir in green onions and garnish with parsley.

Serves 4-6

Barbados, this "Island in the Sun", is known as "Little England" because of 300 years of British rule.

Roast Leg Of Lamb

This is my recipe for lamb roast.

4½ lb.	leg of lamb	2.1 kg
½ cup	chopped green onions	125 mL
3	garlic cloves, minced	3
2 tsp.	hot pepper sauce	10 mL
2 tbsp.	Worcestershire sauce	30 mL
½ tsp.	salt	2 mL
½ tsp.	black pepper	2 mL
½ tsp.	thyme	2 mL
½ tsp.	paprika	2 mL

1. Wash leg of lamb. Make deep slits into meat on both sides.
2. Combine green onions with garlic, hot pepper sauce, Worcestershire sauce, salt, pepper, thyme and paprika. Mix well.
3. Fill slits with mixture and rub remainder on outside of meat. Let stand for 1 hour.
4. Bake at 350°F (180°C), covered with foil, for about 2 hours. Slice and serve with roast potatoes.

Serves 6-8

St. Lucia, like neighbouring islands Martinique and St. Vincent, consist almost wholly of volcanic rock. The northern part of the island is worn down by erosion, the central part is mountainous and the southern part is a flat, coastal plain of alluvial soil.

Pepperpot

Guyana

This national dish of Guyana is derived from the Amerindians. Casareep is a thick syrup obtained from boiled cassava juice *. It is seasoned with salt, pepper, brown sugar, cinnamon and cloves and is considered a preservative for meat. Casareep is now bottled and sold commercially.

2 lbs.	cubed lean beef or pork	1 kg
½ lb.	cut up salt beef	250 g
2	pig trotters, in small pieces	2
1	cow heel, quartered	1
1 lb.	pig's tail, disjointed	500 g
1	lime	1
½ cup	casareep *	125 mL
2	hot peppers	2
1	stick of cinnamon	1
3	cloves	3
2 tbsp.	brown sugar	30 mL
	salt to taste	

1. Wash meat with lime juice. Set aside.
2. Boil cow's heel and pig trotters with enough water to cover meat. When half-cooked, about 1 hour, add other meats and casareep, simmer for another hour.
3. Add remaining ingredients; simmer gently until meats are tender and sauce thick, about 1 hour. Serve hot with boiled rice.

Serves 8-10

* Casareep is the ingredient which gives the dish a distinctive taste. It is available in West Indian grocery stores.

Note: *Pepperpot develops more flavour if left for a few days, but it must be boiled up every day.*

Garlic Pork

Guyana

This dish is Portuguese in origin. Traditionally served at Christmas in Guyana it has also been adopted by some of the other islands.

4 lbs.	cubed pork	2 kg
1	lime	1
2 cups	white vinegar	500 mL
¼ lb.	garlic, crushed (about 4 heads)	125 g
1 tsp.	chopped fresh thyme	5 mL
2	hot peppers, chopped	2
1 tbsp.	salt	15 mL
4	cloves	4
	oil for frying	

1. Wash cubed pork with the juice of a lime; place in an earthenware jar or crock.
2. Mix vinegar with garlic, thyme, hot pepper, salt and cloves. Pour over pork and completely cover with liquid.
3. Refrigerate, covered, for 2 days. Remove pork from marinade. Heat oil in frying pan and fry pork until brown, about 10 minutes. Serve hot.

Serves 6-8

Grenada is known as the "Spice Island of the West", the air is fragrant with the smell of cinnamon, vanilla, ginger and nutmeg. Almost a third of the world's spices are grown on this island.

Stuffed Leg Of Pork

A special occasion dish that looks impressive and has a wonderful aroma and flavour.

4 lbs.	boned pork leg	2 kg
1 tsp.	salt	5 mL
1	lemon	1
1 cup	bread crumbs	250 mL
2	onions, chopped	2
2	garlic cloves, minced	2
½ tsp.	thyme	2 mL
1	hot red pepper, chopped	1
2	celery stalks, chopped	2
½ cup	white wine	125 mL
2 tbsp.	butter OR margarine	30 mL
1 tsp.	black pepper	5 mL
	pineapple slices	

1. Rub leg of pork with ½ tsp. (2 mL) salt and juice of a lemon. Let stand for 30 minutes.
2. Combine bread crumbs with onion, garlic, thyme, hot pepper, celery and white wine.
3. Wash pork leg; season with mixture of butter, salt and pepper. Fill with bread stuffing, roll and tie up firmly.
4. Bake, covered with foil, at 325°F (160°C) for about 2 hours. Uncover and baste with drippings, continue to cook until meat is brown, about 30 minutes. Garnish with pineapple slices and serve.

Serves 6-8

Antiqua, an island of beautiful beaches, was a major U.S. base during the Second World War.

Breads

Roti Or Parathas

Roti, Dahl Puri, Alu Puri are breads brought by the East Indians to the Caribbean. They are enjoyed by all nationalities.

2½ cups	**all-purpose flour**	**625 mL**
2 tsp.	**baking powder**	**10 mL**
1 tbsp.	**butter**	**15 mL**
	water, approximately ¾-1 cup	
	(175-250 mL)	
1 cup	**oil**	**250 mL**

1. Sift 2 cups (500 mL) of flour, add baking powder and butter, mix well. Add water, knead, make a soft elastic, but not sticky dough. Cut into 6 pieces.
2. Roll each piece of dough thinly on a floured board, apply oil to dough surface, sprinkle lightly with a pinch of flour. Fold in half, then quarter, roll up into a ball. Let stand for 10 minutes.
3. Roll out each piece thinly again, place on a baking hotplate, griddle, or tawa. Brush each side of dough with oil to prevent sticking, turn frequently.
4. Remove roti and clap with both hands until pliable. Fold and place on greaseproof paper. A clean towel may be used instead of bare hands for clapping. Serve hot with meat or vegetable curry.

Yields 6 Roti

Dahl Puri
(Split Pea-Stuffed Bread)

Guyana & Trinidad

In Trinidad, the size of this very popular bread is double the size made in Guyana.

1 cup	yellow split peas	250 mL
3 cups	water	750 mL
	salt and pepper to taste	
1 tsp.	hot chili powder (cayenne)	5 mL
1	small onion, chopped	1
1	garlic clove, minced	1
1 tsp.	ground cumin	5 mL
2 cups	flour	500 mL
1 tsp.	baking powder	5 mL
1 tbsp.	butter OR margarine	15 mL
	oil	

1. Wash peas, boil with 2 cups (500 mL) of water mixed with salt, pepper, chili powder, onion and garlic. Reduce heat and simmer, covered, until peas are tender and water evaporated.
2. Grind peas in a mill while hot; add cumin, mix well. Let cool.
3. Sift flour and baking powder together, mix with butter and enough water to make a soft dough.
4. Divide peas and dough into 10 ping-pong-sized balls. Roll out dough to about 3" (7 cm) in diameter, put a ball of peas in centre, flatten, then enclose it with dough.
5. Roll out thinly and cook on heated griddle or tawa, brushing with oil on both sides. Cook until lightly brown and risen.

Yields 10 Puri

See photograph on back cover.

Alu Puri
(Potato-Stuffed Bread)

Guyana

This is also a favourite roti.

1 lb.	potatoes, peeled	500 g
	salt and pepper to taste	
¼ cup	finely chopped green onions	50 mL
1 tsp.	hot pepper sauce	5 mL
1 tsp.	ground cumin	5 mL
2 cups	flour	500 mL
1 tsp	baking powder	5 mL
1 tbsp.	butter OR margarine	15 mL
	water, approximately ¾ cup (175 mL)	
	oil	

1. Cut potatoes in small pieces and boil until tender. Drain then mash. Add salt, pepper, green onions, pepper sauce and cumin. Let cool.
2. Sift flour and baking powder, mix with butter and enough water to make a soft elastic dough.
3. Divide potatoes and dough into 10 ping-pong-sized balls. Roll out dough to about 3" (7 cm) in diameter, brush with oil, put a ball of potatoes in centre, flatten, encase with dough.
4. Roll out thinly, cook on heated griddle or tawa, brushing with oil on both sides. Cook until lightly brown and risen.

Yields 10 Puri

Johnny Cakes

A popular bread used in the Caribbean.

¾ lb.	flour (1 ½ cups [375 mL])	375 g
1 tsp.	baking powder	5 mL
¼ tsp.	salt	1 mL
1 tsp.	shortening	5 mL
1 tsp.	butter	5 mL
½ cup	cold water	125 mL
	oil for deep frying	

1. Combine flour, baking powder and salt. Sift.
2. Rub in shortening and butter and mix with enough water to make a soft dough.
3. Roll dough out to ½" (1.3 cm) thick, cut in rounds with a biscuit cutter. Heat oil to 365°F (185°C). Fry dough rounds in hot oil. Serve immediately.

Makes 8-10

Note: *In Trinidad coconut milk is used instead of water and Johnny Cakes are not fried. Bake for 20 minutes in a hot oven 400°F (200°C). Slice and butter cakes when hot. Serve immediately.*

Montego Bay, tourist capital of Jamaica because of its excellent beaches, is served by an international airport built on reclaimed swamp land.

Bakes

Bakes are usually found at a creole breakfast.
Delicious with saltfish or with any meal.

2 cups	flour	500 mL
2 tsp.	baking powder	10 mL
1 tbsp.	butter	15 mL
½ tsp.	salt	2 mL
2 tsp.	sugar	10 mL
2	eggs	2
½ cup	milk	125 mL
½ cup	water	125 mL
	oil for frying	

1. Sift flour and baking powder. Rub in butter, salt and sugar.
2. Combine mixture with eggs and milk and enough water to make a soft pliable dough. Knead.
3. Break off pieces of dough, roll into balls; flatten into circles about ¼" (1 cm) thick and 4" (10 cm) in diameter. Heat oil to 365°F (185°C). Fry Bakes in hot oil until golden. Drain; serve warm.

Yields 10 Bakes

See photograph opposite page 64.

Corn Bread

1 cup	flour	250 mL
¼ cup	sugar	50 mL
1½ tbsp.	baking powder	22 mL
¾ tsp.	salt	3 mL
1 cup	yellow cornmeal	250 mL
¼ cup	butter	50 mL
1 cup	milk	250 mL
2	eggs, well beaten	2

1. Combine flour, sugar, baking powder and salt. Stir in cornmeal.
2. Cream butter until light, gradually blend in flour mixture. Add milk and eggs. Mix well, beating until smooth.
3. Pour into a greased loaf pan and bake at 375°F (190°C) for 20-30 minutes. Slice and serve with butter, tasty with any meal.

Yields 1 loaf

Bara-Yeast Bread

This split pea yeast bread is another favourite recipe in the Caribbean.

1½ tsp.	yeast	7 mL
½ cup	warm water	125 mL
1 tsp.	sugar	5 mL
1½ cups	all-purpose flour	375 mL
½ cup	ground yellow split peas	125 mL
½ tsp.	paprika	2 mL
1 tsp.	chili powder	5 mL
2	garlic cloves, minced	2
	salt and pepper to taste	
1 tbsp.	butter	15 mL
	oil for frying	

1. Mix yeast with warm water and sugar. Let stand and allow to rise, about 10 minutes.
2. Mix flour, split pea powder, seasonings, and butter with yeast mixture. Knead dough and form into a ball. Let stand for 1 hour.
3. Divide dough into small pieces and roll each out to a diameter of 5" (13 cm). Heat oil to 365°F (185°C). Fry bread in deep fat until golden brown. Drain on absorbent paper.

Yields about 20

St. Lucia claims to possess the only drive-in volcano in the world since the Sulphur Springs in a volcanic crater can be reached by car.

Floats

Fried biscuits are an important part of the traditional Trinidadian dish which is salt fish cakes and floats.

¼ cup	warm water	50 mL
½ tsp.	sugar	2 mL
1 tsp.	dry yeast	5 mL
2 cups	flour	500 mL
½ tsp.	salt	2 mL
⅓ cup	butter OR margarine	75 g
½ cup	warm water	125 mL
	oil for deep-frying	

1. Pour warm water into a bowl, sprinkle with sugar and yeast. Stir to dissolve. Set aside.
2. Mix flour, salt and butter well, until crumbly.
3. Add yeast and enough warm water to flour mixture to make a soft dough. Knead well. Cover and leave in a warm place until mixture doubles in size, about 1 hour.
4. Cut dough into pieces, roll into small balls about 1½" (4 cm) in diameter. Let rise again for about 35 minutes. Heat oil to 365°F (185°C). Roll out the dough balls and fry in hot oil until golden brown. Drain on paper towels.

Yields about 12 Floats

Trinidad is one of the oldest oil producing countries in the world; the first oil well being drilled in 1867.

Desserts

Guyana Black Cake

Guyana

This rich moist cake is served at weddings and at Christmas.

1 lb	raisins	500 g
½ lb.	currants	250 g
¼ lb.	prunes	125 g
1 cup	rum	250 ml
1½ lbs.	brown sugar, packed (3¼ cups [800 mL])	1.5 kg
½ lb.	butter	250 g
6	eggs, beaten	6
½ lb.	flour (1 cup [250 mL])	250 g
½ tsp.	baking powder	2 mL
1 tsp.	mixed spice (nutmeg, cinnamon, cloves, allspice)	5 mL
¼ lb.	mixed peel	125 g
¼ lb.	choppped nuts (optional)	125 g

1. Wash and dry fruit. Grind fruit and soak with ¾ cup (175 mL) of rum. Store, covered, in glass jar to steep for 3 weeks or longer.
2. To make caramel, heat 1 lb. (500 g) of sugar in a heavy-bottomed frying pan until melted; simmer until dark brown. Let cool.
3. Cream butter and ½ lb. (250 g) sugar well, add beaten eggs a little at a time; add soaked fruits and rum, stirring well, and enough caramel to make it as dark as desired.
4. Add sifted flour with baking powder and mixed spice. Fold in peel and chopped nuts.
5. Pour mixture into baking pan, greased and lined with waxed paper. Bake in a slow oven at 300°F (150°C) for about 2-2½ hours.
6. Sprinkle additional rum over cake immediately after it is baked. Repeat a few times. Allow cake to remain in pan for 2-3 days.

Icing For Black Cake

MARZIPAN:

2	egg whites	2
½ lb.	ground almonds (1 cup [250 mL])	250 g
½ lb.	icing (confectioner's) sugar (1 cup [250 mL])	250 g
½ tsp.	almond essence (extract)	2 mL

1. Beat egg whites to a stiff froth, stir in ground almonds, sugar and almond essence to make a paste.
2. Remove cake from pan, place on a cake plate. Cover top of cake with almond paste. Roll rest of paste thinly to cover sides. Allow to dry 1 day before icing.

ROYAL ICING:

2	egg whites	2
1 lb.	icing (confectioner's) sugar (2 cups [500 mL])	500 g
	juice of 1 lemon	

1. Beat egg whites to a froth, add sugar, a little at a time, beating well after each addition. Add lemon juice and sugar and continue to beat until mixture forms peaks.
2. Dip a spatula in hot water and smooth the icing over the almond paste. A second layer may be applied when the first is thoroughly dried.
3. Decorate as desired. If cake is for a wedding choose appropriate colours and decorations. If cake is for Christmas colours chosen may be red and green on white with a Christmas theme.

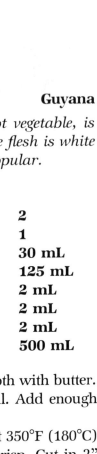

Cassava Pone

Guyana

Cassava, a tropical starchy, root vegetable, is covered with a bark-like skin, the flesh is white and hard. This dessert is very popular.

2	medium sweet cassava	2
1	small, dried coconut	1
2 tbsp.	butter OR margarine	30 mL
½ cup	sugar	125 mL
½ tsp.	allspice	2 mL
½ tsp.	salt	2 mL
½ tsp.	vanilla essence (extract)	2 mL
2 cups	water	500 mL

1. Peel, wash and grate cassava. Grate coconut. Mix both with butter.
2. Add sugar, spice, salt and vanilla essence. Mix well. Add enough water to bind mixture.
3. Bake in a shallow, greased 8" (20 cm) square pan at 350°F (180°C) for about 1-1½ hours. Top should be brown and crisp. Cut in 2" (5 cm) squares before serving.

Serves 6-8

See photograph opposite page 96.

Guyana was described by Sir Walter Raleigh as "El Dorado", city of gold.

Salara - Coconut Roll

Barbados & Guyana

Delicious coconut yeast bread.

1 tbsp.	dry yeast	15 mL
¼ cup	warm water	50 mL
¼ cup	sugar	50 mL
1 cup	milk	250 mL
¼ cup	shortening	50 mL
1 tsp.	salt	5 mL
3 cups	flour	750 mL
1	egg, beaten	1
1 tbsp.	butter	15 mL
1	egg white	1

FILLING:

1 cup	shredded coconut	250 mL
½ cup	sugar	125 mL
½ tsp.	cinnamon	2 mL
½ tsp.	vanilla essence	2 mL
5	drops strawberry food colouring	5

1. Dissolve yeast in warm water. Sprinkle with 1 tsp. (5 mL) of sugar. Mix and let stand
2. Warm milk, combine shortening, salt and sugar; add flour and egg. Knead to make a moderately stiff dough. Shape into a ball.
3. Place dough in a greased bowl, cover; let rise to double in size for about 1 hour. Punch down, divide in half. Roll each half into a 12" x 8" (30 cm x 20 cm) rectangle, brush with melted butter.
4. Combine all filling ingredients and let stand for 1 hour.
5. Sprinkle half of filling mixture on each rectangle of dough. Roll up lengthwise, seal edge.
6. Cover and let rise until double in bulk.
7. Brush rolls with beaten egg white. Bake at 375°F (190°C) for 20-30 minutes. Cut into slices and serve.

Yields 2 rolls

Lil's Shortbread

This delicious recipe was given to me by a friend.

1 cup	soft butter	250 mL
½ cup	brown sugar	125 mL
2¼ cups	flour	550 mL

1. Cream butter and sugar gradually, but thoroughly.
2. Add flour to creamed mixture, ¼ cup (50 mL) at a time, mixing well after each addition.
3. Divide dough into several portions. Flatten 1 portion at a time on a lightly floured surface to ¼" (1 cm) thickness.
4. Cut in desired shapes with floured cutters and place on an ungreased baking sheet.
5. Bake at 325°F (160°C) for 15-20 minutes or until golden brown.

Rice Pudding

The East Indians call this dish Kheer.

1 cup	raw white rice	250 mL
3 cups	water	750 mL
1 cup	evaporated milk	250 mL
1 cup	condensed milk	250 mL
2 tbsp.	raisins	30 mL
½ tsp.	crushed cardamom seeds	2 mL
½ tsp.	grated nutmeg	2 mL

1. Wash rice well. Combine rice and water, bring to a boil and cook on medium heat for about 30 minutes, stirring constantly.
2. Add evaporated milk, condensed milk, raisins and spice; keep simmering for about 30 minutes, stirring frequently to prevent sticking.
3. Pour rice into a baking dish and bake at 350°F (180°C) for about 30 minutes.

Serves 6-8

Trifle

This popular island dessert has British origins.

1	sponge cake, cut in 1" (2.5 cm) cubes	1
¼ cup	sherry	50 mL
1 cup	evaporated milk	250 mL
2 cups	whole milk	500 mL
½ cup	condensed milk	125 mL
6	eggs	6
1 tbsp.	custard powder	15 mL
¼ cup	milk	50 mL
2 tsp.	vanilla essence (extract)	10 mL
2 tbsp.	rum	30 mL
2 cups	cubed fruit (mango, papaya, peaches, pears, etc.)	500 mL
2	pineapple slices, cubed	2
¼ cup	crushed peanuts	50 mL
1 cup	whipping cream, whipped	250 mL

1. Place cubed sponge cake in a bowl and sprinkle with sherry. Set aside.
2. Combine all 3 milks, bring to a boil. Remove from heat, add slightly beaten eggs. Return to low heat, stirring constantly. Dissolve custard powder in milk; add to eggs; keep stirring until custard becomes thick. Cool, add vanilla and rum.
3. Cover bottom of serving dish with half of custard. Arrange soaked cake pieces over custard. Spread fruit cocktail and pineapple pieces over cake. Sprinkle with peanuts. Pour on remaining custard. Refrigerate until custard is set. Top with whipped cream. Refrigerate until serving time.

Serves 10-12

Mango Mousse

Curaçao

A light, refreshing elegant dessert and easy to prepare!

1 tbsp.	gelatin	15 mL
¼ cup	water	50 mL
1 cup	water	250 mL
¼ tsp.	salt	1 mL
½ cup	sugar	150 mL
2 cups	mango purée *	500 mL
6 tbsp.	lime juice	90 mL
1 cup	whipping cream, whipped	250 mL
2 tbsp.	Curaçao	30 mL
	whipped cream for garnish	

1. Sprinkle gelatin over ¼ cup (50 mL) of water and set aside to soften.
2. Bring 1 cup (250 mL) of water to a boil in a small saucepan. Stir in salt and sugar until sugar is dissolved. Remove from heat and stir in gelatin mixture. Cool.
3. In a large bowl, combine mango purée, lime juice and gelatin mixture. Blend thoroughly and refrigerate until partially set.
4. Whip cream until stiff. Beat in Curaçao and fold cream into chilled mango mixture. Refrigerate for several hours or overnight.
5. Garnish with whipped cream.

Serves 6-8

* To make mango purée, lay mango flat, cut a thick slice off the top and then turn mango over and repeat. Scoop pulp out of slices with a spoon. Cut remaining mango pulp away from stones and purée pulp in a blender or food processor.

Coconut Ice Cream

Ice cream is very popular throughout the Caribbean. It can be made with any of the local fruits added to a basic egg custard.

1	dry coconut, grated	1
4 cups	milk	1 L
2 tbsp.	custard powder	30 mL
2	eggs	2
	sugar to taste	
½ tsp.	almond essence (extract)	2 mL

1. Grate coconut; warm 1 cup (250 mL) of milk and pour over grated coconut. Let stand for a few minutes. Squeeze to extract fluid. Strain. Set aside.
2. Heat 2½ cups (625 mL) of milk. Remove from heat. Add custard powder creamed with ½ cup (125 mL) of milk. Return to heat, stirring constantly until mixture thickens. Remove from heat.
3. Beat eggs lightly with sugar and almond essence; pour hot custard over egg mixture, whipping well. Add coconut milk. Mix and cool.
4. Freeze using an ice cream maker according to manufacturer's directions or use freezer tray method. With the freezer tray method, freeze ice cream mixture for 2 hours, remove from freezer, beat thoroughly, refreeze for 2 hours. Repeat beating and freezing twice more to obtain the best ice cream consistency.

Serves 6-8

Variations: *Add 1 cup (250 mL) fruit purée to basic egg custard instead of coconut milk. Try mango, papaya, banana or soursop.*

See photograph opposite page 96.

Index

INDEX

INDEX

GIVE A TASTE OF THE CARIBBEAN

"CARIBBEAN CUISINE" is $10.95 per book plus $1.50 (total order) for shipping and handling.

Number of books _____ x $10.95 = _____

Add shipping and handling charge _____ = $ ____$1.50

Subtotal _____ = $ _____

In Canada add 7% GST_____ (Subtotal x .07) = $ _____

Total enclosed _____ = $ _____

U.S. and international orders payable in U.S. funds / Price is subject to change.

NAME_____

STREET_____

CITY_____ PROV. STATE _____

COUNTRY_____ POSTAL CODE/ZIP_____

Please make cheque or money order payable to:
Betty K Books & Food
3 - 1750 The Queensway
Suite 1305
Etobicoke, Ontario
M9C 5H5

For fund-raising or volume purchases, contact **BETTY K BOOKS & FOOD** for volume rates. Please allow 3-4 weeks for delivery.

GIVE A TASTE OF THE CARIBBEAN

"CARIBBEAN CUISINE" is $10.95 per book plus $1.50 (total order) for shipping and handling.

Number of books _____ x $10.95 = _____

Add shipping and handling charge _____ = $ ____$1.50

Subtotal _____ = $ _____

In Canada add 7% GST_____ (Subtotal x .07) = $ _____

Total enclosed _____ = $ _____

U.S. and international orders payable in U.S. funds / Price is subject to change.

NAME_____

STREET_____

CITY_____ PROV. STATE _____

COUNTRY_____ POSTAL CODE/ZIP_____

Please make cheque or money order payable to:
Betty K Books & Food
3 - 1750 The Queensway
Suite 1305
Etobicoke, Ontario
M9C 5H5

For fund-raising or volume purchases, contact **BETTY K BOOKS & FOOD** for volume rates. Please allow 3-4 weeks for delivery.